# DINOSAURS

Sky Pony Press books may be purchased in bulk at special discounts for sales promotion, corporate gifts, fund-raising, or educational purposes. Special editions can also be created to specifications. For details, contact the Special Sales Department, Sky Pony Press, 307 West 36th Street, 11th Floor, New York, NY 10018 or info@skyhorsepublishing.com.

Sky Pony® is a registered trademark of Skyhorse Publishing, Inc.®, a Delaware corporation.

Visit our website at www.skyponypress.com.

10 9 8 7 6 5 4 3 2 1

Manufactured in China, March 2015
This product conforms to CPSIA 2008

Library of Congress Cataloging-in-Publication Data

Mertz, Leslie A., author.
Dinosaurs / Leslie Mertz.
pages cm
Audience: Ages 8-12
Audience: Grades 4 to 6
Includes bibliographical references and index.
ISBN 978-1-63220-436-3 (hc : alk. paper)
1. Dinosaurs--Juvenile literature. I. Title.
QE861.5.M47 2015
567.9--dc23
2015006634

Cover design by Georgia Morrissey
Cover photo credit: Thinkstock

Ebook ISBN: 978-1-63220-819-4

# FACT ATLAS

# DINOSAURS

## WALK IN THE FOOTSTEPS OF THE WORLD'S LARGEST LIZARDS

**Leslie Mertz**

Sky Pony Press
New York

# Contents

# In the Footsteps of Dinosaurs

**A**s you step into your backyard, onto a ball field, or along a trail in a nearby forest, you might be setting down your foot in the same place that a dinosaur once did. If you happen to live in the eastern United States, that dinosaur could have been the 25-foot-long duck-billed dinosaur called *Hadrosaurus* or the 60-foot-long and 30-foot-tall *Astrodon*, a plant eater that had a heavy body and walked on four legs. Maybe you've walked in Mongolia's Gobi Desert, where the swift little predator *Velociraptor* roamed, or perhaps you've been to Patagonia in South America, where the mightiest beasts ever to walk the Earth shook the ground with massive footsteps. The fact is, you may be walking in the footsteps of dinosaurs on all of the continents. That includes Antarctica, where, despite the frigid landscape there now, scientists have already discovered eight species of dinosaurs.

What an amazing place Earth was in the days of these mighty reptiles! While standing here today, we can only imagine the scene: mammoth plant-eating dinosaurs, some probably in herds, grazing in a forest-surrounded meadow, while packs of small but fast and smart meat-eating dinosaurs looked for an opportunity to attack . . . and the whole scene turned upside down as a bloodthirsty predator like *Tyrannosaurus rex* burst out of the forest and charged! Welcome to the world of the dinosaurs, vanished now but for the efforts of scientists, museums, and your own imagination.

# What's a Dinosaur?

You probably know what reptiles are: snakes, lizards, crocodiles, and turtles are all reptiles. Dinosaurs were reptiles, too, and had a reptile's scaly skin and other reptilian features.

But dinosaurs belonged to one particular group of reptiles. Even though scientists only have fossils (living matter turned into rock or which left an impression in rock) to identify dinosaurs, they have been able to find clear differences between dinosaurs and other reptiles.

One of the most obvious differences is the way dinosaurs walked. The vast majority of dinosaurs walked on legs right under their bodies. Because of this, most of the four-legged dinosaurs walked more like horses, with the legs below the body, than like crocodiles, with their legs spread out to the sides. The two-legged dinosaurs also walked on legs under their bodies, like ostriches.

A turtle is a kind of reptile, but it isn't a dinosaur. All dinosaurs were reptiles, but not all reptiles are dinosaurs.

Left: An ostrich's two legs are directly beneath its body (unlike a turtle's, which splay out to the sides). Most dinosaurs stood the same way as ostriches.
Below: Some dinosaurs had feathers, although none could fly like modern birds.

## DID YOU KNOW?

Many scientists believe that dinosaurs are the ancestors of birds. If that's the case, not all dinosaurs became extinct 65 million years ago. Some survived to give rise to birds, and birds are indeed modern-day dinosaurs!

## WHAT'S IN A NAME?

THE ANIMALS THAT ARE ALIVE TODAY often have both common names and scientific names: black bear is a common name, and *Ursus americanus* is the animal's scientific name. We know dinosaurs only by their scientific names, which are typically written in italics. The scientific name usually comes from the Latin or Greek word for a particular feature of the animal, from the place where it was found, or from a person who was involved in the discovery. As an example, *Edmontosaurus* is a combination of Edmonton, Canada, where the creature's fossils were uncovered, and *saurus*, the Greek word for "lizard."

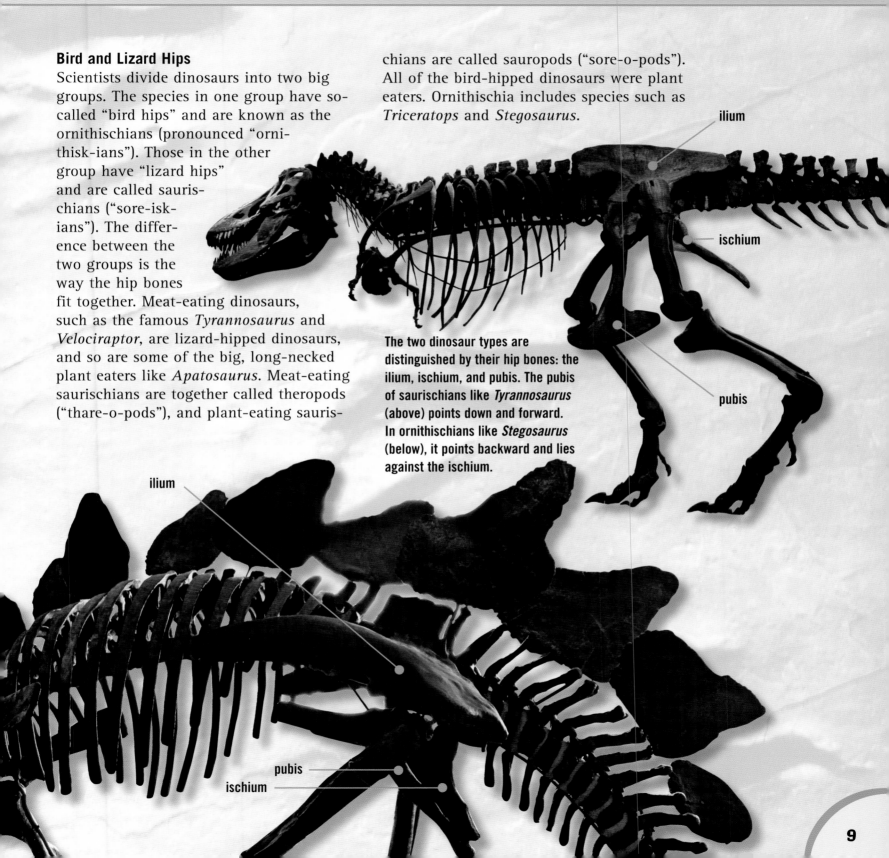

## Bird and Lizard Hips

Scientists divide dinosaurs into two big groups. The species in one group have so-called "bird hips" and are known as the ornithischians (pronounced "orni-thisk-ians"). Those in the other group have "lizard hips" and are called sauris-chians ("sore-isk-ians"). The differ-ence between the two groups is the way the hip bones fit together. Meat-eating dinosaurs, such as the famous *Tyrannosaurus* and *Velociraptor*, are lizard-hipped dinosaurs, and so are some of the big, long-necked plant eaters like *Apatosaurus*. Meat-eating saurischians are together called theropods ("thare-o-pods"), and plant-eating sauris-

chians are called sauropods ("sore-o-pods"). All of the bird-hipped dinosaurs were plant eaters. Ornithischia includes species such as *Triceratops* and *Stegosaurus*.

ilium

ischium

The two dinosaur types are distinguished by their hip bones: the ilium, ischium, and pubis. The pubis of saurischians like *Tyrannosaurus* (above) points down and forward. In ornithischians like *Stegosaurus* (below), it points backward and lies against the ischium.

pubis

ilium

pubis

ischium

# The Age of Dinosaurs

**A**bout 250 million years ago, something happened—nobody knows what—that caused nine of every ten plant and animal species to die off.

Some of the few animals that survived this great extinction were reptiles. Without much competition from other animals, reptiles began to evolve into many new species, including the dinosaurs. Dinosaurs appeared on the planet about 230 million years ago in the Triassic period.

## Earth During the Age of Dinosaurs

The number of dinosaur species increased during the Triassic period when the climate was warm and dry, but dinosaurs really took off in the Jurassic period, when the climate became more humid. They continued to thrive in the tropical climate of the Cretaceous period, after the first flowering plants appeared. Flowering plants were good for the dinosaurs. Not only were they tasty to the plant-eating species, but they also provided food for insects and other animals that then became dinner for the meat-eating dinosaurs. The dinosaurs did so well during the Jurassic and Cretaceous periods that they became the dominant animals on the planet. Today, scientists refer to the dinosaurs' reign on Earth as the Age of Dinosaurs.

## Why Did They Go Extinct?

Scientists aren't sure exactly why dinosaurs vanished 65 million years ago. Most think that one or more of the following contributed to the extinction:

1. **A large asteroid (a rock from space) smashed into Earth** and sent massive plumes of dust and debris into the air, blocking the sun, and causing very sudden shifts in Earth's climate.

2. **Disease killed off the dinosaurs.**

3. **Dinosaurs couldn't find enough food** because mammals started eating the same things as the dinosaurs.

4. **The slow movement of the continents on Earth**—called continental drift—caused the climate to change, and the dinosaurs could not adjust to the new conditions.

5. **Some of the mammals developed a taste for dinosaur eggs** and ate so many that too few dinosaur babies hatched.

*Herrerasaurus* appeared in the late Triassic period.

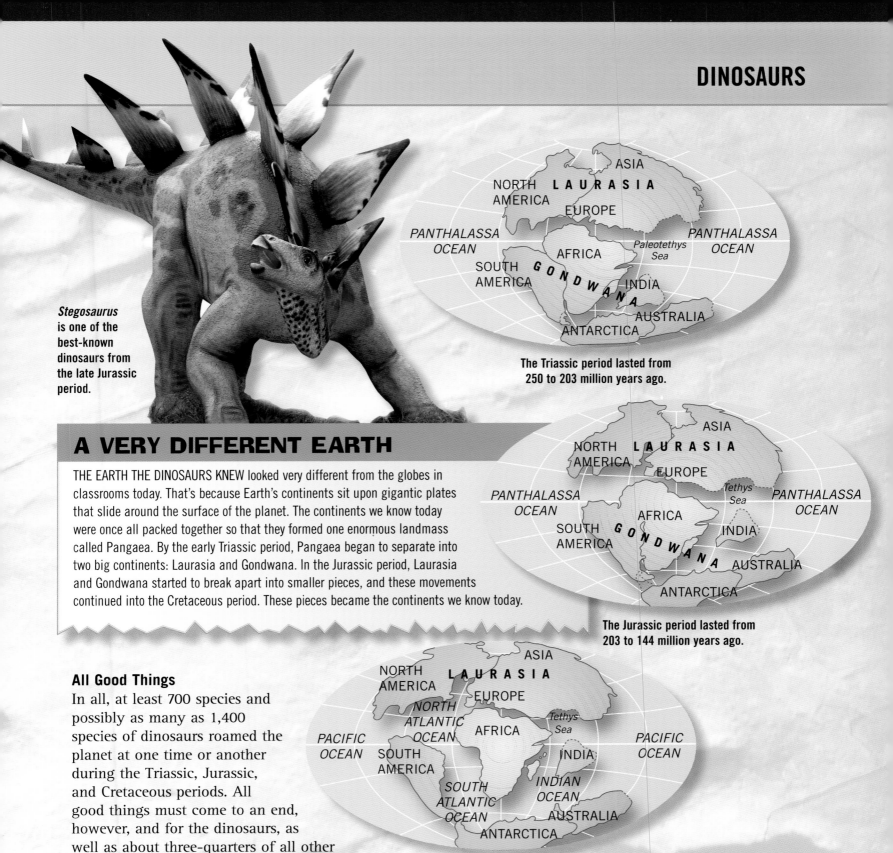

*Stegosaurus* is one of the best-known dinosaurs from the late Jurassic period.

The Triassic period lasted from 250 to 203 million years ago.

## A VERY DIFFERENT EARTH

THE EARTH THE DINOSAURS KNEW looked very different from the globes in classrooms today. That's because Earth's continents sit upon gigantic plates that slide around the surface of the planet. The continents we know today were once all packed together so that they formed one enormous landmass called Pangaea. By the early Triassic period, Pangaea began to separate into two big continents: Laurasia and Gondwana. In the Jurassic period, Laurasia and Gondwana started to break apart into smaller pieces, and these movements continued into the Cretaceous period. These pieces became the continents we know today.

The Jurassic period lasted from 203 to 144 million years ago.

### All Good Things

In all, at least 700 species and possibly as many as 1,400 species of dinosaurs roamed the planet at one time or another during the Triassic, Jurassic, and Cretaceous periods. All good things must come to an end, however, and for the dinosaurs, as well as about three-quarters of all other species on Earth, the end came 65 million years ago, when they became extinct.

The Cretaceous period lasted from 144 to 65 million years ago.

# Digging Dinosaurs

 **W**hat exactly is a fossil? Fossils are the bones, teeth, or other remains of a plant or an animal that have hardened into rock. Fossils may also be impressions of such material left in rock—like a handprint in concrete. Turning plant or animal material into rock—a process called fossilization—takes many, many years. The fossils of dinosaurs that we find today, for instance, come from animals that lived 230 to 65 million years ago.

The chances of a dinosaur's bones becoming fossils were extremely low. Conditions had to be just right. First, the dinosaur had to die someplace where predators or scavengers wouldn't have a chance to eat it. Second, it had to die in such a way that the animal's body and bones wouldn't decay and disappear. This usually means that the dinosaur had to be completely buried in moist mud or sand at the time of its death, or soon after.

Something like this could have happened during a flood: an animal might drown, sink, and get covered up by fine sand or muck carried in the floodwater. As years passed, more and more sand and mud would cover the animal, burying it farther and farther down. Over millions of years, the bones would turn into stone and become fossils.

A paleontologist carefully uncovers a dinosaur claw, now a fossil.

## DINOSAUR HUNTING FOR TWO CENTURIES

ALTHOUGH PEOPLE HAVE FOUND fossils of dinosaurs for many thousands of years, it has only been a little more than 150 years that we have known what they were. In fact, the word *dinosaur* didn't exist until 1841. That's when a fossil expert, or paleontologist ("pay-lee-on-tol-o-jist"), named Richard Owen combined the Greek words *deinos*, which means "terrible," and *saurus*, which means "lizard," to create the term *dinosaur*. Now that we know what to look for, we've found dinosaur fossils in the United States, Canada, China, South America, Africa, and other locations around the world—and you can see them in museums just about everywhere.

**Richard Owen lived from 1804 to 1892 and was an expert on the animal kingdom.**

## HOW OLD IS THAT DINOSAUR?

YOU KNOW HOW OLD YOU ARE because you know when your birthday is. It's not so easy with dinosaurs. Scientists usually figure out the age of a dinosaur fossil by the age of the rock around it. The deepest rock layers are usually the oldest. One way to date a rock layer is to look for fossils of other plants or animals that are already known to have lived at a certain time. If they are there, scientists can assume that the dinosaur fossils contained in the same layer are the same age.

Another way to learn the age of the fossil is to measure the radioactivity of any lava rock that is nearby. The more ancient the lava rock, the less radioactive it is. If lava rock above the fossil is 150 million years old, and a layer beneath it is 170 million years old, the scientists can say that the fossil is between 150 and 170 million years old.

Above: When paleontologists discover a dinosaur bone, they set up a dig site. They divide the area into squares and work carefully to unearth the rest of the dinosaur.

Below: The dark band marks the K-T boundary between the Cretaceous (K) and the Tertiary (T) periods. The lighter rock below it belongs to the Age of Dinosaurs. Above it lie more recent rock layers.

# To the Moon

Today, one part of northwestern Argentina, an area called Ischigualasto ("Ish-thee-goo-ah-lasto"), is a dry and rugged landscape full of bright red sandstone and mudstone (rock made of sand and mud). It looks so unusual that it is known as the Valley of the Moon. It wasn't always this way. Back about 230 million years, in the late Triassic period—the days of the earliest dinosaurs—it was a lush river valley, occasionally suffering from the effects of volcanic eruptions. Trees standing more than 120 feet tall dotted the landscape, and plants would grow especially thick during the yearly wet season.

Paleontologists are very interested in the Valley of the Moon because it is the only known place on the planet that displays a complete collection of rock layers for the entire Triassic period. This means that it may hold fossils that tell the whole history of the early dinosaurs. Finds from the Valley of the Moon may help scientists solve the long-standing mysteries of what the ancestors of the dinosaurs looked like and how the dinosaurs would eventually become the rulers of the animal world.

# Dawn of Dinosaurs

In 1988, world-renowned fossil hunters Paul Sereno and Fernando Novas uncovered a nearly complete skeleton of *Herrerasaurus* in the Valley of the Moon, Argentina. At the time, *Herrerasaurus* was the oldest known dinosaur.

Three years later, Sereno returned to the same place with several students. One of them, named Ricardo Martinez, discovered a fossilized skull and skeleton, which turned out to belong to dinosaurs even older than *Herrerasaurus*. Paleontologists now know this ancient dinosaur as *Eoraptor*.

**Eoraptor** shared many features with later theropods, including walking on two legs, balancing with a long tail, and carrying its head on a slender neck. But **Eoraptor** had five fingers (later cousins had only two or three) and leaf-like, instead of pointed, teeth.

Found in the soil in the Valley of the Moon, the backbone and upper limbs of an *Eoraptor* emerge.

## The Oldest Dinosaur?

After studying the fossil, Sereno reported that it had the features that they would have expected in a primitive dinosaur: it was small (only about 3 feet long), it walked on two legs, and it ate meat. He speculated that it probably ate animals smaller than itself, and may also have kidnapped the babies of larger dinosaurs, killing and eating them after it fled.

## DINO DATA

### EORAPTOR LUNENSIS

**SCIENTIFIC NAME:** *Eoraptor lunensis*

**MEANING OF NAME:** *Eoraptor* means "dawn stealer." *Lunensis* means "of the moon," referring to the discovery of the fossil in the Valley of the Moon, Argentina.

**SIZE:** Up to 36–40 inches long

**WEIGHT:** About 20 pounds

**WHEN IT LIVED:** 230 million years ago (Triassic)

**DESCRIPTION:** Carnivorous, but may have sometimes eaten plants, too. Walked on two long, hind legs, perhaps occasionally on all fours. Likely a fast-running predator.

**FIERCE FACTS:** One of the oldest dinosaurs known, possibly the oldest. May be the ancestor of other dinosaurs.

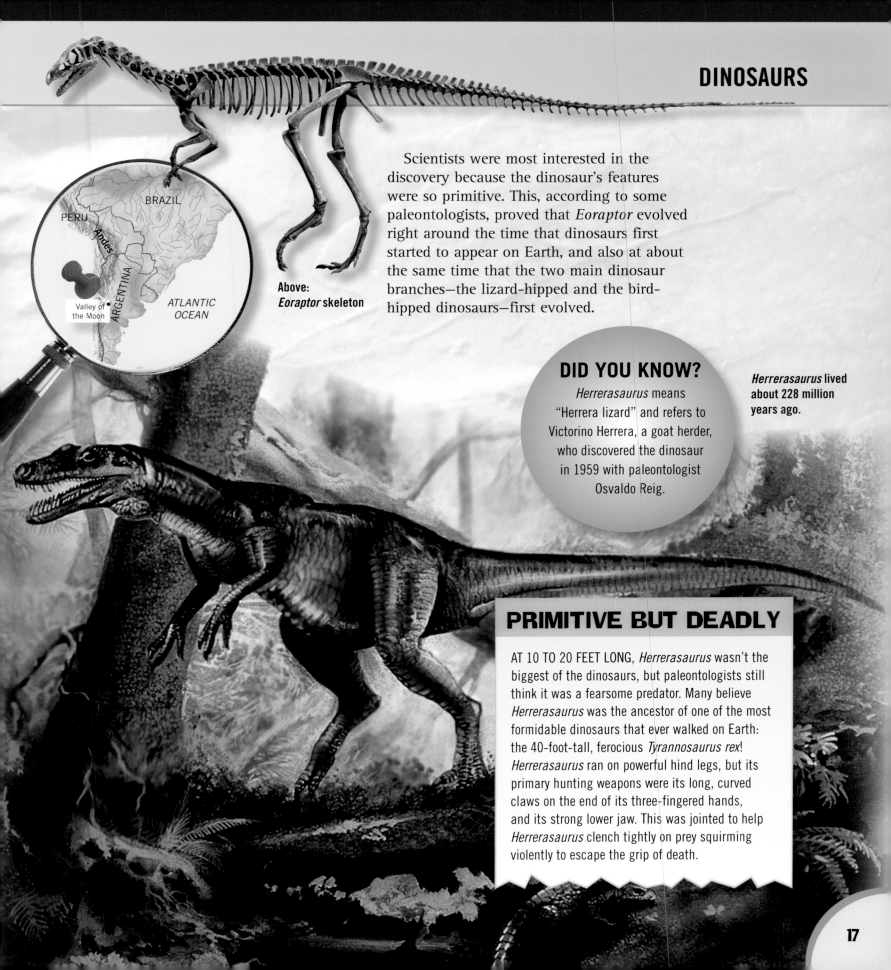

PERU

BRAZIL

Andes

ARGENTINA

Valley of
the Moon

ATLANTIC
OCEAN

**Above:**
*Eoraptor* skeleton

Scientists were most interested in the
discovery because the dinosaur's features
were so primitive. This, according to some
paleontologists, proved that *Eoraptor* evolved
right around the time that dinosaurs first
started to appear on Earth, and also at about
the same time that the two main dinosaur
branches—the lizard-hipped and the bird-
hipped dinosaurs—first evolved.

## DID YOU KNOW?

*Herrerasaurus* means
"Herrera lizard" and refers to
Victorino Herrera, a goat herder,
who discovered the dinosaur
in 1959 with paleontologist
Osvaldo Reig.

*Herrerasaurus* lived
about 228 million
years ago.

## PRIMITIVE BUT DEADLY

AT 10 TO 20 FEET LONG, *Herrerasaurus* wasn't the
biggest of the dinosaurs, but paleontologists still
think it was a fearsome predator. Many believe
*Herrerasaurus* was the ancestor of one of the most
formidable dinosaurs that ever walked on Earth:
the 40-foot-tall, ferocious *Tyrannosaurus rex*!
*Herrerasaurus* ran on powerful hind legs, but its
primary hunting weapons were its long, curved
claws on the end of its three-fingered hands,
and its strong lower jaw. This was jointed to help
*Herrerasaurus* clench tightly on prey squirming
violently to escape the grip of death.

17

# Big . . . Bigger . . . Biggest!

In 1990, a team of paleontologists led by Rodolfo Coria headed to South America's Patagonia region to search the fossil-rich, exposed rocks for dinosaurs. They soon found one in Argentina that was larger than any other known dinosaur. Coria and fellow paleontologist José F. Bonaparte named it *Argentinosaurus*.

With that discovery, *Argentinosaurus* took the title as the biggest dinosaur that ever lived. From the tip of its outstretched snout to the end of its tail, it measured 120 to 130 feet—about the length of three school buses parked in a row.

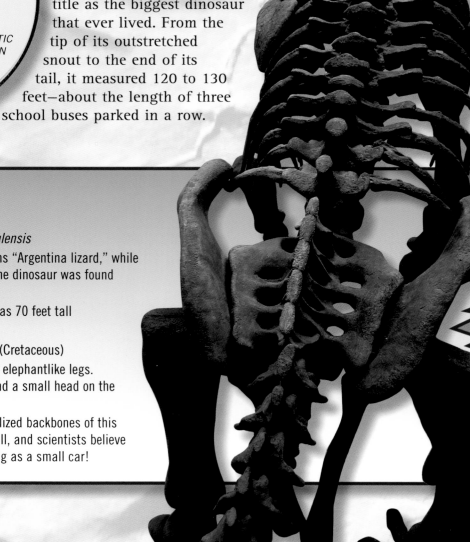

A reconstruction of an *Argentinosaurus* skeleton, on display at Atlanta's Fernbank Museum of Natural History. Fairly few fossilized bones have been excavated, so scientists have to make educated guesses about how a whole skeleton would look.

## DINO DATA

### *ARGENTINOSAURUS*

**SCIENTIFIC NAME:** *Argentinosaurus huinculensis*

**MEANING OF NAME:** *Argentinosaurus* means "Argentina lizard," while *huinculensis* refers to the region where the dinosaur was found (Huincul, Argentina).

**SIZE:** 120–130 feet long, possibly as much as 70 feet tall

**WEIGHT:** 100–110 tons

**WHEN IT LIVED:** 100–85 million years ago (Cretaceous)

**DESCRIPTION:** Herbivorous. Walked on four, elephantlike legs. An enormous dinosaur with a long tail and a small head on the end of a long neck.

**FIERCE FACTS:** Many of the individual fossilized backbones of this massive creature stand at least 4 feet tall, and scientists believe its shoulder blade would have been as big as a small car!

*Argentinosaurus* weighed as much as twelve elephants combined!

If *Argentinosaurus* swung its neck up, it could reach 40 feet high at least, and possibly as much as 70 feet. That means that if it were alive today, it would be tall enough to peek into a window on the fifth or sixth floor of a building. Its weight was also impressive: between 100 and 110 tons!

## Surviving Later in Patagonia

Paleontologists grew even more excited about *Argentinosaurus* when they learned when it lived. In other parts of the world, the big, long-necked plant eaters—which were sauropods—died out millions of years before the giant carnivores, such as *Tyrannosaurus*, evolved. In Patagonia, however, the sauropods didn't become extinct when the others did. Instead, they got bigger . . . and bigger! And the biggest of them all was *Argentinosaurus*.

### Dino Mystery: Why So Big?

CASE OPEN!

*ARGENTINOSAURUS* GREW UP to 130 feet long and could have gained as much as 100 pounds a day as an adolescent. It was one of many big, long-necked, plant-eating dinosaurs, including such species as *Supersaurus* (up to 112 feet long) and *Brachiosaurus* (up to 82 feet long). Why were these dinosaurs so huge? No one knows for sure. Some scientists think that they grew to such a big size because they had so much food to eat. At that time, the forests were thick with plant life. Other scientists believe that they evolved into such enormous animals as a defense against predators. After all, what predator in its right mind would attack an 80- to 110-ton dinosaur?

# What Big Teeth You Have!

At 6 feet long, the skull of *Giganotosaurus* was longer than most people are tall.

**A**t one time on Earth, a war of the goliaths raged. A fierce dinosaur called *Giganotosaurus*—a predator even larger than *Tyrannosaurus*—hunted down and tore apart the largest dinosaur that ever lived: *Argentinosaurus*.

In 1990, paleontologists found the first fossils of *Argentinosaurus* in Argentina, but they didn't know if giant theropods lived there, too. Then, in 1993, an amateur fossil hunter named Ruben Carolini scanned the ground in Patagonia, Argentina, and found the fossilized remains of what turned out to be an enormous theropod. It was soon named *Giganotosaurus carolinii*.

*Giganotosaurus carolinii* measured about 42 feet long and had a gigantic 6-foot-long skull that held a mouth full of sharp, serrated teeth, some of them 8 inches long. In addition, it could run fast and had sharp, curved claws on the three fingers of each hand. No doubt about it, *Giganotosaurus* was truly a killing machine.

## Pack Hunters and Big Prey

Even though *Giganotosaurus* was colossal by theropod standards, it was still overshadowed by the immense size of *Argentinosaurus*. Scientists think *Giganotosaurus* gained the upper hand by hunting in groups. Such an attack must have been a sight to see as a pack of *Giganotosaurus* dinosaurs chased down, pounced on, and tore into the flesh of the bigger beast until, staggering, *Argentinosaurus* finally fell to the ground with a deafening thud, the pack descending to tear away chunks of meat.

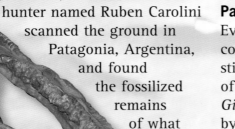

*Giganotosaurus*

## DINO DATA

### GIGANOTOSAURUS CAROLINII

**SCIENTIFIC NAME:** *Giganotosaurus carolinii*

**MEANING OF NAME:** *Giganotosaurus* means "giant southern lizard" and *carolinii* refers to discoverer Ruben Carolini.

**SIZE:** 42–44 feet long

**WEIGHT:** 6–8 tons

**WHEN IT LIVED:**
93–89 million years ago (Cretaceous)

**DESCRIPTION:** Carnivorous. Walked on two legs, with two clawed front arms available for seizing and slicing into prey. Up to 8-inch-long knifelike teeth filled the mouth of the enormous, 6-foot-long skull.

## DID YOU KNOW?

An Argentinian theropod discovered in 2006, called *Mapusaurus roseae*, may have been even bigger than *Giganotosaurus*. The scientists found fossils of adult *Mapusaurus*—reaching more than 40 feet long—and juveniles, suggesting that these meat-eating beasts lived in families and hunted in packs.

## HORNED KILLER

ANOTHER PREDATOR that lived in Argentina was the 30-foot-long *Carnotaurus*. Its name means "meat-eating bull" and refers to the pair of rather frightening horns that protrude from its forehead. It would have been a fearsome predator, using its strong legs for pursuing prey and rows of bladelike teeth on its jaws to tear flesh to bits.

VENEZUELA

COLOMBIA

ECUADOR

PERU

Andes

*Mapusaurus*

BRAZIL

CHILE

*Giganotosaurus*

PACIFIC
OCEAN

ARGENTINA

URUGUAY

ATLANTIC
OCEAN

*Carnotaurus*
**skeleton, left, and
reconstruction,
above**

# The Wild West

If you want to find dinosaur fossils, one of the best places in the world to look is North America—and the United States in particular. Paleontologists have unearthed the fossils of more kinds of dinosaurs on this continent—most in western deserts and badlands—than anywhere else on the planet. Why? Part of the reason is that paleontologists have spent a lot of time—more than 150 years—searching for dinosaurs in the United States.

One of the first people to begin a study of American fossil dinosaurs was Joseph Leidy, who got a call in 1858 to help identify the very first nearly complete skeleton of a dinosaur that anyone had ever found. Leidy named the dinosaur *Hadrosaurus foulkii*. It was a "duck-billed" dinosaur, so-called because the bones of its skull resembled those seen in today's ducks. The dinosaur itself, however, didn't look much like a duck. It was 25 feet long, ran on two powerful hind legs, dropped down to all fours to munch on plants, and the back of its mouth was full of small teeth. Over his lifetime, Leidy also named several other new species. It was only the start. Scientists have identified hundreds of North American dinosaur species, with more sure to come.

# Mysteries of Ghost Ranch

**This *Coelophysis* has crocodile and other bones in its stomach.**

In 1947, a team from the American Museum of Natural History made an amazing discovery. Buried in the desert at Ghost Ranch, New Mexico, lay hundreds of dinosaurs, all crammed together in one mass grave. Nearly all of the dinosaurs were *Coelophysis*.

## Great Flood

With the discovery of the *Coelophysis* dinosaurs, Ghost Ranch became one of the richest dinosaur fossil sites in the entire world. Where did this sizeable collection of *Coelophysis* come from? From the start, scientists agreed that the dinosaurs had died in a great flood. In the days of *Coelophysis*, that area of New Mexico was a river valley, and the floodwaters and mud would have buried the dinosaurs quickly. But why had so many dinosaurs died together? Some scientists thought at first that *Coelophysis* must have hunted in enormous herds. If so, it would be big news. Certain predators, like modern-day wolves, hunt in packs, but none of them hunt in herds of hundreds and hundreds of animals.

Since then, most paleontologists have decided that the dinosaurs were not traveling in a herd, but were instead simply in the same place at the same time because food was so plentiful in the river valley. With the water teeming with fish and the shoreline drawing other small prey animals, *Coelophysis* would have had a smorgasbord laid out in front of it.

Ghost Ranch, New Mexico

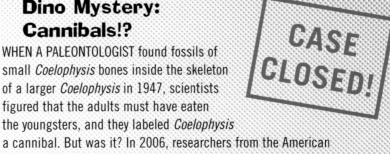

### Dino Mystery: Cannibals!?

WHEN A PALEONTOLOGIST found fossils of small *Coelophysis* bones inside the skeleton of a larger *Coelophysis* in 1947, scientists figured that the adults must have eaten the youngsters, and they labeled *Coelophysis* a cannibal. But was it? In 2006, researchers from the American Museum of Natural History took another look at the small fossil bones and found that they were actually the bones of primitive crocodiles and other unidentified reptiles. The name of *Coelophysis* was cleared: it wasn't a cannibal after all.

**CASE CLOSED!**

## LIGHTWEIGHT KILLER

*COELOPHYSIS* STRETCHED about 6 to 10 feet long and walked on its two hind legs. It only stood about 3 feet tall, however, because it probably tilted its body forward when it moved. Scientists believe it could run faster than many other dinosaurs of its size. Its jaws were long and pointed and filled with dozens of sharp teeth that were serrated on both sides, rather like a two-sided saw. Its arms were short, but each was tipped with three sharp claws. *Coelophysis* killed its prey swiftly. In fact, pound for pound, *Coelophysis* was one of the most vicious predators among all the dinosaurs.

# American Sauropods

In 1859, a geologist (somebody who studies rocks) named John Macomb led an expedition into the rugged canyons of western North America. There, in what we now know as the state of Utah, one of his men found a few enormous fossilized bones. It took a while to figure out what they were, but in 1877 scientists realized they had found a sauropod. It was the first time that a fossil from one of these long-necked, long-tailed, plant-eating dinosaurs had been discovered in North America.

**A *Camarasaurus* herd, complete with young. Paleontologists think many sauropod species may have traveled in herds or family groups.**

It wasn't long before paleontologists learned that this sauropod was not alone. On digs in the western United States, they found a number of different sauropods, all of which lived from about 156 to 145 million years ago, in the Jurassic period. Today, scientists have a long list of American sauropods. It includes: *Apatosaurus*, which grew as long as 70 feet (about two school buses put together), *Camarasaurus* (65 feet long), *Diplodocus* (maybe as much as 110 feet long), *Supersaurus*, which reached an astonishing 108 to 112 feet long, and many others.

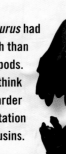

**_Camarasaurus_ had tougher teeth than most sauropods. Paleontologists think it ate woodier (harder to chew) vegetation than its cousins.**

## DINO DATA

### CAMARASAURUS

**SCIENTIFIC NAME:** *Camarasaurus*

**MEANING OF NAME:** *Camarasaurus* means "chambered lizard," referring to the holes, or chambers, in its backbones.

**SIZE:** 60–65 feet long

**WEIGHT:** 20 tons

**WHEN IT LIVED:** 155–145 million years ago (Jurassic)

**DESCRIPTION:** Herbivorous. Its four, elephantlike legs supported a tail and neck that were long, but not as long as those of most other sauropods. Its short snout gave its head a rounded appearance.

**FIERCE FACTS:** *Camarasaurus* was one of several dinosaurs that scientists once thought had too small a brain to serve such a large body. They even thought these dinosaurs had a second brain near the hips! They now know that they didn't, which is too bad— how many brains would you like to have if you could?

Sauropods like *Apatosaurus* needed to eat a lot. In fact, they probably ate nearly every waking minute to feed their huge frames.

## BONE WARS

FOR SEVERAL DECADES starting in 1868, the fossil beds of the American West were the focus of an intense competition between two paleontologists, Othniel Charles Marsh and Edward Drinker Cope. The pair tried to sabotage each other's fossil digs, spied on each other's progress, and even planted fossils in fossil-free locations to make the other team waste time digging. Despite the nasty rivalry, Cope and Marsh between them discovered a total of more than 120 new dinosaur species, including several sauropods. Marsh named *Apatosaurus* in 1877— the same year that Cope named *Camarasaurus*.

Edward Cope

Othniel Marsh

## Dino Mystery: Whip It Good!

**CASE OPEN!**

*APATOSAURUS* HAD A 45-FOOT-LONG TAIL, and popular opinion once held that the dinosaur used it to whip its enemies to protect itself. Studies of its tailbones showed, however, that they were just too small and fragile to make a good weapon. Now scientists think that the dinosaur probably snapped its tail to make a cracking noise that could reach an astounding 200 decibels, which is louder than the noise made by a jet engine! (You can make a similar sound—though much quieter!—by snapping a twisted-up, wet towel.) Why did *Apatosaurus* make such a loud sound? Experts have suggested several reasons:

1. To find a mate
2. To scare off attackers
3. To settle scuffles among themselves

# The Best Defense

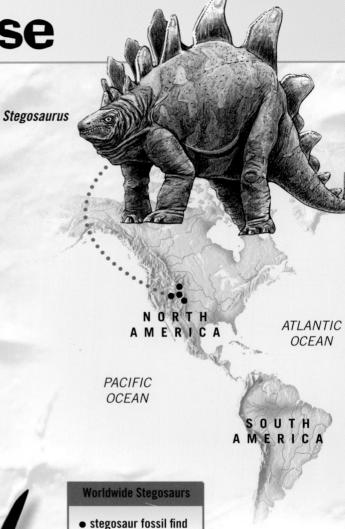

*Stegosaurus*

As a beefy, slow-moving plant eater, *Stegosaurus* must have made quite a target for the awesome predators that lived nearby. Living at the end of the Jurassic period about 150 million years ago, *Stegosaurus* didn't even have front teeth to protect itself; instead it had a beak. How did it survive when it lived alongside 15- to 20-foot-long, horned *Ceratosaurus* dinosaurs, 40-foot-long *Allosaurus* dinosaurs, and roaming packs of smaller but vicious predators?

Some scientists think one answer may have involved the double row of tall, finlike plates that ran from the back of the neck all the way down the tail. They believe that the plates acted like armor and protected *Stegosaurus* from the teeth and claws of predators. Other scientists doubt that idea because *Stegosaurus* only had plates on the top of its back.

**The tail of *Stegosaurus* may have been its best defense.**

**N O R T H   A M E R I C A**

*PACIFIC OCEAN*

*ATLANTIC OCEAN*

*S O U T H   A M E R I C A*

**Worldwide Stegosaurs**

● stegosaur fossil find

They argue that a predator would find it quite simple to avoid the plates altogether and rip chunks off the meaty sides of *Stegosaurus*.

Most paleontologists do agree, however, that *Stegosaurus* used its tail to defend itself. Although its tail was not especially long, it came ready-made with four sharp spikes. Think of it like the thorns on a rose—that is, if the thorns were 3 feet long! A swipe from that tail may well have been enough to convince an attacker to look elsewhere for lunch.

**Kentrosaurus** may have reared up on its hind legs to nibble on those hard-to-reach leaves on the tops of trees.

EUROPE

ASIA

ICA

Stegosaur fossils have been found on four continents.

## Other Stegosaurs

*Stegosaurus* is actually only one kind of stegosaur. Other members of the group known as Stegosauria include such dinosaurs as:

- *Kentrosaurus,* a 16.5-foot-long and 700-pound dinosaur from Africa that had tall spikes instead of plates and an extra set of spikes at its shoulders. It lived about 156 to 150 million years ago.

- *Paranthodon,* which probably looked much like *Kentrosaurus.* It was of the first dinosaurs discovered in Africa. It lived about 145 to 138 million years ago, possibly making it the last surviving stegosaur on Earth.

- *Huayangosaurus,* a 13-foot-long, 660-pound dinosaur from China with plates and tail spikes, as well as a pair of long shoulder spikes. It is one of the most primitive stegosaurs and lived about 165 million years ago, or about 15 million years before *Stegosaurus.*

## Dino Mystery: Two-Footed?

CASE OPEN!

Stegosaurs had front legs that were shorter than the back legs, just like *Tyrannosaurus* and *Allosaurus.* Does that mean that they all walked on two legs? *Tyrannosaurus* and *Allosaurus* did, but stegosaurs spent most of their time on all fours. Scientists think some stegosaurs, like *Kentrosaurus* (which had particularly short front legs), could probably rear up on its hind legs from time to time to nip leaves off of trees. They aren't so sure about *Stegosaurus.* Some think it could raise its front legs off the ground, but others doubt it.

# Nightmare Dragon

**Even as a skeleton, *Allosaurus* is frightening. Its apparent ferocity has earned it the nickname, the Nightmare Dragon.**

**W**estern North America looks very tame today compared to the late Jurassic period. *Allosaurus* is one very big reason why. Its 40-foot-long body made it one of the region's largest predators. In addition, it had dozens of curved, 4-inch-long teeth with edges like a serrated steak knife, and its jaw could swing open very widely, like a python's. Some scientists believe that *Allosaurus* charged at its prey with its mouth completely open, impaled the prey with its teeth, and then sawed through the flesh, tearing off huge chunks of meat, which the predator then swallowed whole.

Over the years, paleontologists have found *Allosaurus* teeth marks on the fossilized bones of prey animals, including *Apatosaurus*, which was one of the largest sauropods in North America. They have also discovered *Allosaurus* teeth mixed in with the fossilized bones of its prey. In other words, *Allosaurus* fed so ferociously that its teeth actually came out of its mouth in the fury of attacking and slicing the meat off its prey. This was not a problem for *Allosaurus*, however, because new teeth would grow in to replace them.

Scientists think that *Allosaurus* occasionally dined on already-dead carcasses, but that it was also fully capable of chasing down and killing most dinosaurs of its time. This predator ran up to 20 miles per hour—an amazing feat for a beast that tipped the scales at 1.5 to 2 tons. (The fastest humans can run only a little bit faster, but they weigh less than 200 pounds!) Besides its speed and its rows of teeth, *Allosaurus* could also use the three, curved claws on each of its short but strong front legs to inflict considerable damage.

**Allosaurus tooth**

## DINO DATA

### ALLOSAURUS FRAGILIS
**SCIENTIFIC NAME:** *Allosaurus fragilis*

**MEANING OF NAME:** *Allosaurus* means "different lizard." *Fragilis* means "fragile" and refers to the neck and some of the back bones, which had hollow spaces in them.

**SIZE:** Up to 40 feet long

**WEIGHT:** 1.5–2 tons

**WHEN IT LIVED:** 156–145 million years ago (Jurassic)

**DESCRIPTION:** Carnivorous. Walked and ran on two powerful hind legs, and used the three, up to 10-inch-long claws on each arm to handle and possibly attack prey. It had a large head with two short horns that stood just above and in front of each eye.

**FIERCE FACTS:** Based on the many fossils of *Allosaurus* dinosaurs that have been found in Colorado, Montana, Utah, and Wyoming, it may have been the most common meat-eating dinosaur of its time.

**Western United States**

● *Allosaurus* fossil finds

Montana

N. Dakota

Idaho

S. Dakota

Wyoming

Nebraska

Nevada

Utah

Colorado

California

Kansas

Arizona

Oklahoma

New Mexico

Texas

An *Allosaurus* discovers a dead dinosaur. Although it was a fearsome predator, *Allosaurus* probably wouldn't turn down a free meal.

## Dino Mystery: A Lonely Hunter?

**CASE OPEN!**

SCIENTISTS BELIEVE that *Allosaurus* had the skill and power to take down a young sauropod single-handedly, but it probably could not have killed a healthy adult. After all, an adult would have been considerably larger than an *Allosaurus*. What if *Allosaurus* hunted in packs—could they then go after adult sauropods? Although scientists still do not have proof, some believe that *Allosaurus* dinosaurs were indeed pack hunters and could have ganged up to kill even large, adult sauropods.

# Feathered Foes

At no more than 7 feet tall and probably adorned with feathers, you might think that *Utahraptor* wasn't much of a predator, but you'd be dead wrong. A larger cousin to *Velociraptor*, *Utahraptor* weighed about 1,500 pounds. It would have carried its massive head about on level with an adult human's. Of course, humans weren't around back then, which is lucky because *Utahraptor*'s jaws were easily large enough to engulf a person's head and a good portion of his or her chest!

*Utahraptor*, discovered in eastern Utah, had big claws on both its hands and its feet, but the giant claw on the second toe was the fiercest. Curved into a perfect slicing tool, it could grow about a foot long. Scientists think that this fast-running carnivore chased down prey with its two, big foot claws drawn up off the ground. Once it was upon its victim, it would swing down its long arms, grabbing the animal with its front claws and at the same time delivering a bite with its sharp, backward-curving teeth. Next, it would turn to the foot-long back claws to slice open the prey's gut. After the slaughter, it would settle down and eat its fill.

*Utahraptor* lived 125 to 120 million years ago in the Cretaceous period, and was a member of a dinosaur family known as Dromaeosauridae. The family includes *Velociraptor* and *Deinonychus*, which were smaller than *Utahraptor* but had similar traits, including the dangerous toe claws. Scientists think one of the dromaeosaurs' ancestors evolved into birds, so *Utahraptor*, *Deinonychus*, and *Velociraptor* are pretty closely related to birds, and scientists suspect that they all had feathers.

*Utahraptor*

## OUR CHANGING PERCEPTIONS

SOME PEOPLE CONSIDER the discovery of *Deinonychus* one of the most important dinosaur finds because it changed the way we view dinosaurs. Until paleontologist John Ostrum described *Deinonychus* in the late 1960s and 1970s, just about everyone thought that all dinosaurs were sluggish, slow-moving animals. Ostrum, however, painted a picture of *Deinonychus* as an active predator that hunted its prey with speed and agility.

Lions hunt in packs to catch their prey. It's possible that *Deinonychus* did the same.

## BIRDS OF A FEATHER HUNT TOGETHER

ALTHOUGH SCIENTISTS could use more evidence, some think that dromaeosaurs hunted in packs. Part of the reason is that paleontologists found the first fossils of *Deinonychus* grouped together near the fossilized skeleton of an herbivore named *Tenontosaurus*. The scientists believe that a pack of *Deinonychus* dinosaurs attacked the much larger beast but died during the struggle. This pack of dinosaurs may have hunted like African lions sometimes do today, lying in wait and ambushing in a coordinated attack. In this way, a pack of lions can slay much larger animals than an individual lion could if it hunted alone.

### DID YOU KNOW?

*Utahraptor* and other members of its family, Dromaeosauridae, were some of the most intelligent of all dinosaurs. Some scientists believe they were as brainy as bottlenose dolphins, which (besides humans) are the smartest animals alive today.

MT

SD

ID

WY

NE

CO

• Gaston Quarry, Utah

UT

AZ

NM

The teeth of *Deinonychus* slanted backward, allowing it to grip its struggling prey.

# Ancient Tank

Imagine a cross between a tank, a spiny porcupine, and a lizard, and you'll get something similar to the ankylosaur known as *Euoplocephalus*. An adult stood only 4 to 6 feet tall, but it measured 20 to 23 feet long and weighed about 3 tons—that's as much as a typical SUV! Short legs carried its body down low to the ground, keeping the animal short but protected, like a turtle. Many ankylosaurs were covered with natural armor, and even the little 3-foot-tall and 6-foot-long ankylosaur called *Minmi* had small bony plates here and there. On *Euoplocephalus*, however, armor plates almost completely covered its back and tail, and some of the plates had spikes. It even had armor plates that it could slide down over its eyelids. Now that's protection!

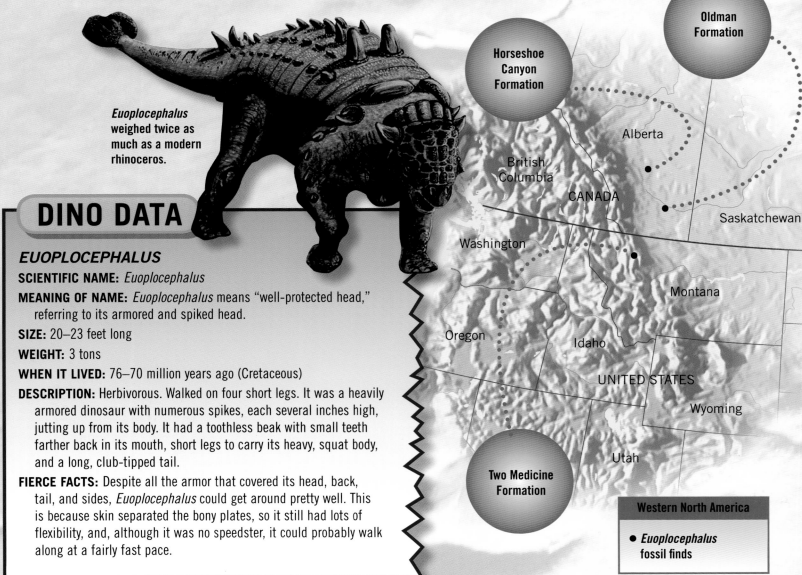

*Euoplocephalus* weighed twice as much as a modern rhinoceros.

## DINO DATA

### *EUOPLOCEPHALUS*

**SCIENTIFIC NAME:** *Euoplocephalus*

**MEANING OF NAME:** *Euoplocephalus* means "well-protected head," referring to its armored and spiked head.

**SIZE:** 20–23 feet long

**WEIGHT:** 3 tons

**WHEN IT LIVED:** 76–70 million years ago (Cretaceous)

**DESCRIPTION:** Herbivorous. Walked on four short legs. It was a heavily armored dinosaur with numerous spikes, each several inches high, jutting up from its body. It had a toothless beak with small teeth farther back in its mouth, short legs to carry its heavy, squat body, and a long, club-tipped tail.

**FIERCE FACTS:** Despite all the armor that covered its head, back, tail, and sides, *Euoplocephalus* could get around pretty well. This is because skin separated the bony plates, so it still had lots of flexibility, and, although it was no speedster, it could probably walk along at a fairly fast pace.

Oldman Formation

Horseshoe Canyon Formation

Alberta

British Columbia

CANADA

Saskatchewan

Washington

Montana

Oregon

Idaho

UNITED STATES

Wyoming

Two Medicine Formation

Utah

**Western North America**

- *Euoplocephalus* fossil finds

## A GOOD SNIFFER

THE 6-FOOT-LONG *SAICHANIA* was another well-armored and heavily spiked ankylosaur. In addition to all this protection, it may have found another way to defend itself from predators: a keen sense of smell. Scientists have found thin swirls of bone inside its nose. These swirls look a lot like the bones seen today in the noses of mammals, which can pick up scents very well. A good sense of smell would have helped *Saichania* get a whiff of approaching animals, including predators, and given them time to hightail it to safety.

The bony body armor of ankylosaurs included everything from spikes (like *Edmontonia*, left), to lumps (like *Pinacosaurus*, below).

### Power Hitters

Another unusual feature of *Euoplocephalus*, and a few other ankylosaurs, was the big bony club at the end of its tail. The club was actually a fused lump of tailbones and armor plates. The tails of the plant-eating *Euoplocephalus* and its larger relative, *Ankylosaurus*, didn't lash like a whip but instead swayed back and forth stiffly, like a baseball bat. To get an idea of how the tail moved, imagine a baseball player warm up by swinging a bat with a heavy doughnut-shaped weight on the end. If you think a smack with that doughnut would hurt, imagine the clubbed tail on a 3-ton *Euoplocephalus* or a 4-ton *Ankylosaurus*! A strike with one of their tails would probably have crushed bones.

A fossilized *Euoplocephalus* tail. A blow with this could cripple—or even kill—an attacker.

# Duck Dinosaurs

**E**dmontosaurus is one of the largest of the hadrosaurs, or duck-billed dinosaurs, so named because hadrosaur skulls look a great deal like those of modern-day ducks. Of course, a duck the size of *Edmontosaurus* would reach almost from home plate on a baseball diamond to the pitcher's mound.

The skull of the typical hadrosaur flattened out in front to form a ducklike beak. The dinosaur used its beak to nip off leaves,

**Like most hadrosaurs, *Edmontosaurus* could walk on either all fours or on its hind two legs alone.**

- North Slope, Alaska

*migration route*

INLAND
SEA

**N O R T H   A M E R I C A**

- Hell Creek, Montana

- Javelina Formation, Texas

***Edmontosaurus* fossil finds from Alaska to Texas led some researchers to suggest these hadrosaurs migrated. If so, other dinosaurs likely migrated also, perhaps seasonally.**

## DINO DATA

### EDMONTOSAURUS

**SCIENTIFIC NAME:** *Edmontosaurus*

**MEANING OF NAME:** *Edmontosaurus* means "Edmonton lizard," and refers to Edmonton, Canada, where it was first discovered.

**SIZE:** Up to 43 feet long

**WEIGHT:** 3.5–4.5 tons

**WHEN IT LIVED:** 76–65 million years ago (Cretaceous)

**DESCRIPTION:** Herbivorous. Walked on four legs, with the rear pair taller and much more beefy than the front pair. It had a long tail at one end and a head with a decidedly duck-shaped bill at the other.

**FIERCE FACTS:** In 1908, a fossil-hunting family—a father and three boys—found an *Edmontosaurus* mummy (a corpse becomes a mummy if its skin or organs dry out but don't decay) in Wyoming. This mummy included almost the entire, intact skeleton; a considerable amount of perfectly preserved skin; and even some of the muscle.

stems, and pine needles from forest plants and trees. Unlike present-day ducks, hadrosaurs could also chew their food with thousands of teeth, stacked row upon row on the sides of the jaws.

One hadrosaur, called *Parasaurolophus*, is known for the large crest on its head. Its crest was a hollow tube of bone that curved out and over the dinosaur's back and grew as much as 6 feet long. Since *Edmontosaurus*, *Parasaurolophus*, and other hadrosaurs didn't have claws or armor to defend themselves, they likely traveled in big herds and may have had other means of defense. *Parasaurolophus* may have used its crest like a bullhorn, warning others if it saw a predator!

## A *Parasaurolophus* Crest

SCIENTISTS THINK *PARASAUROLOPHUS* may have used its crest for one or more of three different jobs:

**1.** All *Parasaurolophus* would have needed was a glimpse of the crest to make sure that an approaching dinosaur was another *Parasaurolophus*. In addition, the differences in each dinosaur's crest may have helped dinosaurs identify each other— many scientists think that males and females had differently sized crests, and that the crests grew longer as the dinosaurs grew older.

**2.** The crest may have kept the brain from overheating.

**3.** *Parasaurolophus* may have been able to blow air through its crest to make a loud sound. The sound of bellowing dinosaurs must have been a strange but fantastic symphony!

*Parasaurolophus*

## Dino Mystery: A Good Parent?

**CASE OPEN!**

SOME SCIENTISTS take the discovery of *Maiasaura* eggs that were almost ready to hatch as proof that this hadrosaur was a good parent. They say that the babies inside the eggs were so undeveloped—much like human infants are when they are born—that the young dinosaurs would not have been able to feed themselves after they hatched and would have needed their parents. Other paleontologists, however, have looked at the babies' skeletons and think they may have been strong enough to make it on their own almost as soon as they were born.

**Did *Maiasaura* care for its young? Many creatures—including most birds, the dinosaurs' only living relatives— feed and protect their infants.**

# Horns and More

**O**ne of the most easily identified dinosaurs is *Triceratops*. With a large frill that rose from the back of the head, up to two-yard-long horns that poked forward from the forehead, and a body length twice that of a rhinoceros, it is hard to confuse *Triceratops* with anything else.

## A Pointed Question

What was the purpose of the horns and the frill? Scientists still aren't certain. Surely, *Triceratops* dinosaurs could have used their long brow horns to defend themselves against attacks by predators, but as yet, scientists have no definite proof that they did. Some paleontologists

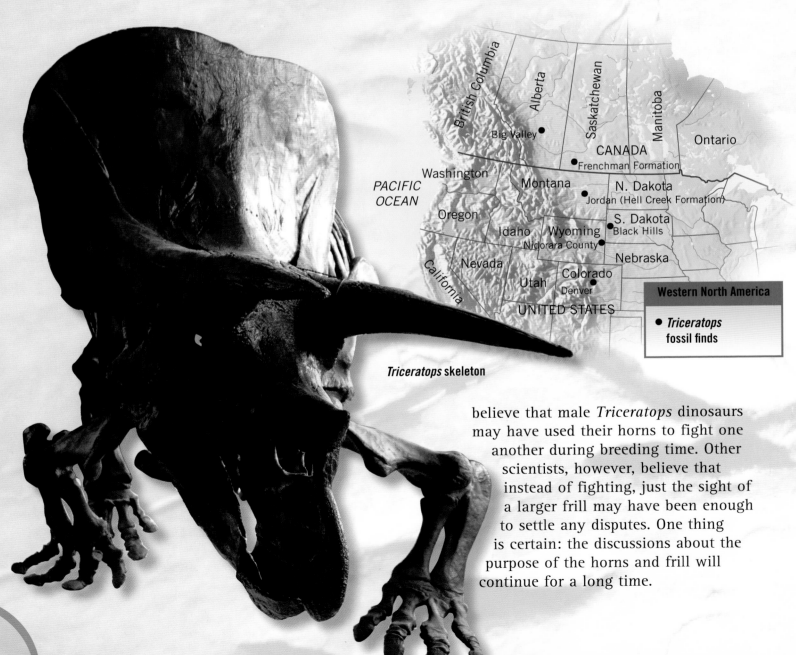

*Triceratops* skeleton

PACIFIC OCEAN

British Columbia

Alberta

Big Valley

Saskatchewan

Manitoba

CANADA
Frenchman Formation

Ontario

Washington

Montana

N. Dakota
Jordan (Hell Creek Formation)

Oregon

Idaho

Wyoming
Niobrara County

S. Dakota
Black Hills

Nebraska

California

Nevada

Utah

Colorado
Denver

UNITED STATES

**Western North America**

● *Triceratops*
fossil finds

believe that male *Triceratops* dinosaurs may have used their horns to fight one another during breeding time. Other scientists, however, believe that instead of fighting, just the sight of a larger frill may have been enough to settle any disputes. One thing is certain: the discussions about the purpose of the horns and frill will continue for a long time.

## Frilly Family

*Triceratops* wasn't the only dinosaur with a bony frill. Other members of its family, the ceratopsians, also had frills. So did dinosaurs from another closely related family, called protoceratopsians. Two of these frilled ceratopsian dinosaurs were *Styracosaurus* and *Centrosaurus*. *Styracosaurus* had a shorter frill than *Triceratops*, but its frill was edged with a number of prominent horns. This 18-foot-long dinosaur had three facial horns just as *Triceratops* did, but *Styracosaurus*'s central horn was longer than the two above the eyes. *Centrosaurus* looked much like *Styracosaurus*, but its frill only had little horny nubs along its edge. *Centrosaurus* grew to as much as 16 feet long.

## BIGGEST SKULL EVER

THE LARGEST SKULL EVER found on a land-living animal belonged to *Pentaceratops*. Just a bit smaller than *Triceratops* in body length, the skull of *Pentaceratops* was more than 3 feet longer than that of *Triceratops*. In all, its skull measured almost 10 feet long—that's more than one-third of its entire body length. Imagine how big your head would be if it were one-third of your height. It would reach down to nearly your chest!

Despite the name, which means "five-horned face," *Pentaceratops* only had three real horns.

## DINO DATA

### TRICERATOPS

**SCIENTIFIC NAME:** *Triceratops*

**MEANING OF NAME:** *Triceratops* means "three-horned face," referring to the two long horns over the eyes and the smaller horn above the nose.

**SIZE:** Up to 30 feet long

**WEIGHT:** Up to 6 tons

**WHEN IT LIVED:** 67–65 million years ago (Cretaceous)

**DESCRIPTION:** Herbivorous. This bulky beast walked on all four legs rather like a present-day rhinoceros. It had a big, parrotlike beak, a bony frill around its head, and two long and pointed horns that jutted out from above its eyes. These so-called brow horns could reach as long as 3 feet.

**FIERCE FACTS:** Some of the bones in the neck of adult *Triceratops* (as well as other adult ceratopsians) were fused together. This would have made the neck extra strong, and helped support the dinosaur's huge head, which measured up to 6.5 feet long.

Two *Triceratops* join battle against a hungry *Tyrannosaurus rex.*

# King of Tyrant Lizards

**A**t 40 feet long with a thick, heavy tail, a pair of muscular hind legs, and a mighty set of jaws with more than fifty banana-sized teeth, it's easy to see why *Tyrannosaurus rex* has held the human imagination since 1902, when fossil hunter Barnum Brown found the first *Tyrannosaurus rex* skeleton in southeastern Montana. Today, scientists know of at least thirty *Tyrannosaurus* skeletons from the western United States. *Tyrannosaurus* may also have lived in Asia, but several experts think those dinosaurs belong to a different genus, *Tarbosaurus*.

Dinosaur movies often show *T. rex* as a fierce and brutal predator, but scientists have held different opinions over the years. Some believe that

## Dino Mystery: Itty-Bitty Arms

**CASE OPEN!**

SCIENTISTS AREN'T SURE why *Tyrannosaurus* and many other carnivores had such tiny arms. Perhaps they used them to help push themselves up after lying down, but some scientists think tyrannosaurs never laid down, not even to sleep. Maybe tyrannosaurs used their arms, and the sharp claws on their fingers, to grab their prey. Or, possibly, the males used them to help hang onto females while they were mating.

tyrannosaurs (the dinosaur family that includes *T. rex*) were slow, plodding animals that mainly ate already-dead animals they came across or that hid at the forest's edge and ambushed unwary prey that passed nearby. Others, however, think that a tyrannosaur was much too big an animal to survive that way. Instead, they believe *T. rex* was indeed a skilled hunter and a fairly fast runner, reaching speeds up to 25 miles per hour. That may not seem all that speedy, but when you consider that the average adult can run at a speed of just 15 to 17 miles per hour, it's plenty fast.

**Western North America**

• *T. rex* fossil finds

CANADA
Eastend •
ND
Hell Creek •
MT    Badlands
ID        • "Sue"
WY        SD
NE
North Horn Formation
• Golden
UT    CO        KS
• Philmont Scout Ranch
NM

## A DINO NAMED SUE

ONE OF THE MOST FAMOUS tyrannosaurs is a *T. rex* known as "Sue," now on display at the Chicago Field Museum of Natural History. First found in South Dakota in 1990, it is the largest and most complete *T. rex* ever discovered. Sue stands 13 feet tall and stretches 42 feet long.

**Sue the *T. rex***

One of the best-known dinosaurs, *T. rex* was also one of the largest. An adult human wouldn't even reach a *T. rex*'s knee.

## DINO DATA

### *TYRANNOSAURUS*

**SCIENTIFIC NAME:** *Tyrannosaurus*

**MEANING OF NAME:** *Tyrannosaurus* means "tyrant lizard."

**SIZE:** At least 42 feet long, possibly as much as 50 feet long

**WEIGHT:** About 6 tons

**WHEN IT LIVED:** 68–65 million years ago (Cretaceous)

**DESCRIPTION:** Carnivorous. Walked on two powerful legs. It had an odd mix of an enormous set of jaws in a 5-foot-long skull, but two puny 3-foot-long arms.

**FIERCE FACTS:** Along with huge jaws that opened extremely wide—big enough to swallow a human child whole— scientists think *Tyrannosaurus* may have had another advantage while looking for prey: 3-D vision. Humans have 3-D (or binocular) vision, but most dinosaurs didn't. In a tyrannosaur, 3-D vision would have given it depth perception, so it could easily pinpoint how far away a prey animal stood.

# Born in Europe

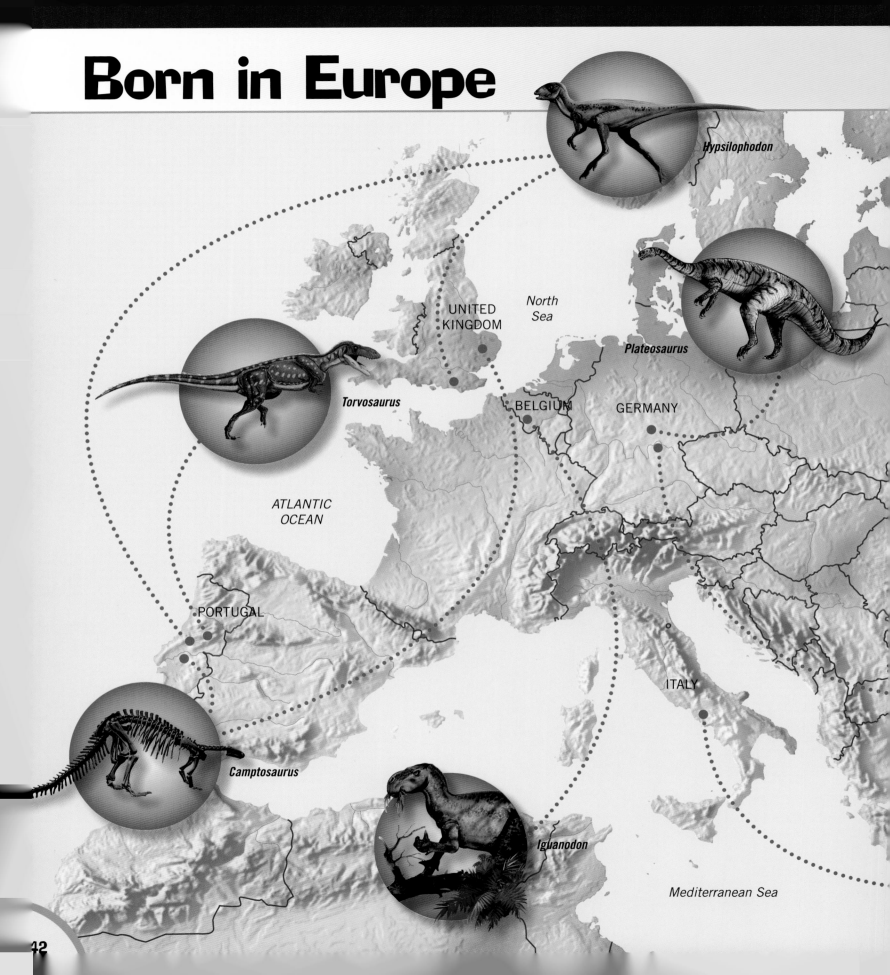

Hypsilophodon

Plateosaurus

North Sea

UNITED KINGDOM

BELGIUM

GERMANY

Torvosaurus

ATLANTIC OCEAN

PORTUGAL

ITALY

Camptosaurus

Iguanodon

Mediterranean Sea

Long before we knew about dinosaurs, people found and collected interesting pieces of stone that looked like enormous bones or that had strange, unnatural-looking imprints. Sometimes, people thought they had found the bones of ancient heroes. Sometimes, they admitted frankly that they didn't know what they were! Once scientists figured out that these unusual stones were actually the fossilized remains of long-dead plants and animals, the field of paleontology was born.

Even though most of the early discoveries were only a few teeth or broken-off pieces of jaw or other bones, scientists began naming the animals and plants. Three of the first animal finds, which were named in the 1820s and 1830s, all came from England. They were the meat-eating *Megalosaurus* and the plant-eating *Iguanodon* and *Hylaeosaurus*.

The new field of paleontology got a major boost in March 1878, when a coal mine in Belgium made history. There, miners working deep in the ground began unearthing fossils—a lot of them. By the time the digging was done, paleontologists had identified more than three dozen fossilized *Iguanodon* dinosaurs.

Other discoveries throughout Europe started pouring in, and the fossil finds have continued to this day. One of the most exciting new discoveries is in Spain, where construction workers accidentally discovered a mass grave . . . containing the fossils of more than 8,000 dinosaurs from 8 different species!

*Archaeopteryx*

*Scipionyx samniticus*

# Giants in the Quarry

In 1824, *Megalosaurus* became one of the first dinosaurs to be named. But its story begins more than 100 years earlier. In the 1670s, Robert Plot, a chemist and museum curator in England, received a fossil that had been collected at a nearby quarry. After carefully studying it, he decided that it was a piece of a thigh bone, broken off not far above the knee. The problem was that this piece of bone was way too big to have come from any known animal. So, Plot proclaimed that it came from a giant man.

No other fossils from this "giant man" surfaced until 1815. In 1818, paleontologist Georges Cuvier took a look at the new bones—discovered in the same quarry as Plot's fossil—and quickly saw that they were the fossilized bones of a huge lizardlike beast. Six years later, paleontologist William Buckland named the beast *Megalosaurus*. Even though the word "dinosaur" wouldn't be invented for nearly twenty years, the name *Megalosaurus* stuck. In fact, the name *Megalosaurus* was such a hit that for a little while, fossil hunters started naming all of the big lizardlike creatures that they found *Megalosaurus*, including many we now know to be completely different species of dinosaurs.

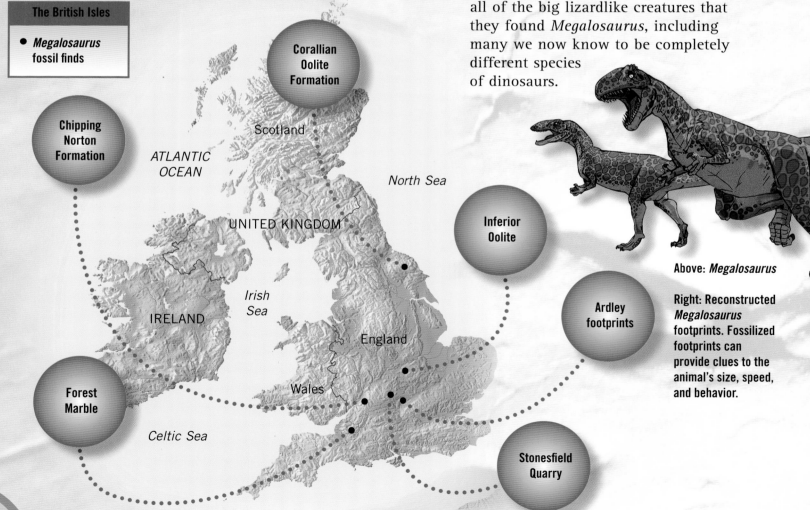

**The British Isles**

- *Megalosaurus* fossil finds

Corallian Oolite Formation

Chipping Norton Formation

Scotland

ATLANTIC OCEAN

North Sea

UNITED KINGDOM

Inferior Oolite

Irish Sea

IRELAND

Ardley footprints

England

Wales

Forest Marble

Celtic Sea

Stonesfield Quarry

Above: *Megalosaurus*

Right: Reconstructed *Megalosaurus* footprints. Fossilized footprints can provide clues to the animal's size, speed, and behavior.

## THE FIRST DINO MUSEUM

BY THE MID-1800s, people really started to get interested in dinosaurs, and the owners of a new museum called the Crystal Palace, located in England, wanted a life-sized model of the meat-eating *Megalosaurus* to display. Sculptor Benjamin Waterhouse Hawkins got the job. He worked with paleontologists to make lifelike models of *Megalosaurus* and other dinosaurs. Although Hawkins and the scientists did their best with *Megalosaurus*, we now know that it wasn't perfect. The model had a large, somewhat crocodile-like head, perched on what looked like a bear's body. The model showed the dinosaur walking on all fours. Today, we know that *Megalosaurus* did have a big head, but the 30-foot-long beast actually walked on its hind two legs, as did *Tyrannosaurus* and other meat-eating dinosaurs.

Hawkins' old-fashioned
*Megalosaurus* statue

## DINO DATA

### MEGALOSAURUS

**SCIENTIFIC NAME:** *Megalosaurus*

**MEANING OF NAME:** *Megalosaurus* means "big lizard" or "great lizard," which simply refers to its large size.

**SIZE:** Up to 30 feet long

**WEIGHT:** Up to 2 tons

**WHEN IT LIVED:** 180–165 million years ago (Jurassic)

**DESCRIPTION:** Carnivorous. Walked on two, burly hind legs. It had a big head, a short, thick but flexible neck; a pair of jaws lined with jagged teeth; and short arms that were armed with sharp claws on the three fingers of each hand.

**FIERCE FACTS:** To keep its big body fed, *Megalosaurus* probably was a good hunter, and may have been able to take down massive, plant-eating sauropods and even stegosaurs. Like other meat eaters, it probably took the easy way out sometimes: if it came across the carcass of a dead animal, it would tear off a hunk of rotting flesh as a between-meal snack.

# The Early Bird

**A**lthough it might seem unlikely, most scientists believe that dinosaurs are the ancestors of the birds that live on Earth today. How did this happen? Every once in a while, a living thing is born with a mutation (a natural but random change) that causes a noticeably odd or rare characteristic. Sometimes, for instance, people may be born with mutations that cause color blindness or that put a dimple in the chin.

## Mutant Dinosaurs!

Mutations happened in dinosaurs, too, and one of those was feathers. Scientists think that a mutation may have caused certain dinosaurs to be born with extra-large scales. For some reason, those extra-large scales turned out to be a good thing—perhaps they helped keep the dinosaurs warm, even during cold weather that killed other dinosaurs. When those big-scaled dinosaurs grew up to have young of their own, their babies had bigger scales, too. Again, those with the biggest scales survived the longest and had the most offspring. Over many, many generations, the scales turned into feathers—and these successful dinosaurs turned into birds.

LAURASIA

GERMANY

ATLANTIC OCEAN

Tethys Sea

GONDWANA

INDIA

## TETHYS SEA

ALL OF THE FOSSILS of *Archaeopteryx* come from the same spot in Germany. In *Archaeopteryx*'s time, however, Germany looked a lot different than it does today: it was a group of warm islands at the edge of an ocean called the Tethys Sea. The sea sat between the only two continents on the planet at the time: Laurasia (now North America, Asia, and Europe) and Gondwana (now Africa, South America, Antarctica, and Australia).

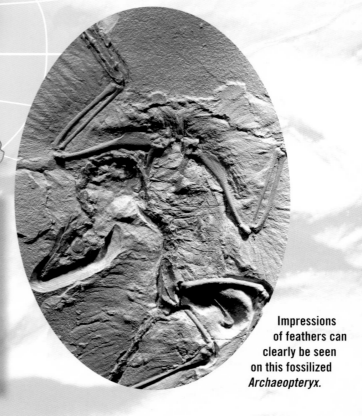

**Impressions of feathers can clearly be seen on this fossilized *Archaeopteryx*.**

## DINO DATA

### ARCHAEOPTERYX

**SCIENTIFIC NAME:** *Archaeopteryx*

**MEANING OF NAME:** *Archaeopteryx* means "ancient feather" or "ancient wing," referring to the feathered wings on this primitive bird.

**SIZE:** Up to 2 feet long

**WEIGHT:** About a pound

**WHEN IT LIVED:** 155–145 million years ago (Jurassic)

**DESCRIPTION:** Carnivorous. Walked on two legs. Other than its wide wings and its feathers, this early bird looked much like a small dinosaur. Scientists aren't sure whether it could flap its wings and truly fly, or if it was only able to hold out its wings and glide.

**FIERCE FACTS:** More evidence that dinosaurs evolved into birds came in 2005, when scientists looked carefully at the toes of *Archaeopteryx*. Instead of one toe on each foot pointing backward and the others forward, like they do in modern birds, the toes of *Archaeopteryx* all pointed forward, just like they do on dinosaur feet.

*Archaeopteryx* might not have flown like modern birds, but it could certainly glide from tree to tree, or from trees to the ground.

### Into the Air

Evidence that dinosaurs evolved into birds came from the discovery of fossils of two ancient animals: *Archaeopteryx* and *Compsognathus*. *Compsognathus* grew to around 3 to 4 feet long and *Archaeopteryx* to about 1.5 to 2 feet long, but other than that, they looked almost identical. The two did have one major difference: *Compsognathus* had only scales on its body, but *Archaeopteryx* had long feathers. Many scientists today believe that *Compsognathus* was an ancestor of birds, and *Archaeopteryx* was one of the first birds, if not the very first bird, to evolve.

*Compsognathus* and a dead *Archaeopteryx*

# The Oldest Iguana

The hand spike looks almost like a human thumb, but it had no joints. *Iguanodon* probably used it for defense or possibly to open tough fruits or seeds.

**L**ike *Megalosaurus, Iguanodon* was one of the first named dinosaurs. Its discovery came in 1822 when paleontologist Gideon Mantell (or possibly his wife) found some big teeth in southern England. Mantell had no idea what kind of animal would have had such large teeth, and he brought them to other scientists to see what they thought. One of them felt the teeth looked like those of a modern-day iguana, which is a lizard that lives in Central and South America. The only problem was that the fossilized teeth were about twenty times larger than the teeth of any known iguana. (If one of your teeth were twenty times bigger, it would be the size of your hand!) Nonetheless, Mantell liked the comparison to an iguana, and he named the owner of the teeth *Iguanodon* (which means "iguana-tooth").

A few years later, Mantell heard about more fossils discovered in a nearby English county. They came from *Iguanodon*, too. From this jumble of fossils, he put together a picture of *Iguanodon*: it was a big animal that walked on all fours, dragging its tail on the ground, and had a cone-shaped horn on the end of its snout. Not everything in Mantell's picture was correct. Paleontologists now believe *Iguanodon* usually walked on two legs, holding its body nearly parallel to the ground, and only dropped down to all fours when it needed to move a little faster. In addition, *Iguanodon*'s tail was stiff, and its "snout horn" didn't fit on the snout at all. Instead, *Iguanodon* had one spike on each hand.

An *Iguanodon*—on all fours to better run away—tries to fend off a pair of attacking *Deinonychus*.

Many modern birds migrate. Some paleontologists think their ancient dinosaur relatives migrated as well.

Clayton Lake, New Mexico

NE

CO

KS

NM

OK

TX

## DINOSAUR MIGRATION

IN 1982, a flood at Clayton Lake in northeastern New Mexico revealed hundreds of 100-million-year-old dinosaur footprints preserved in rock. Most of the tracks probably came from dinosaurs in *Iguanodon*'s family, the ornithopods (bird-feet dinosaurs). Some scientists think Clayton Lake's large number of tracks, and other sites like it, show that dinosaurs migrated much like birds do today—except that the dinosaurs walked instead of flew.

**Western Europe**

● Nineteenth-century *Iguanodon* fossil finds

UNITED KINGDOM

● Maidstone, Kent
● Whiteman's Green, Sussex

● Atherfield, Isle of Wight

BELGIUM

● Bernissart

English Channel

FRANCE

## Dino Mystery: Blood

**CASE OPEN!**

COLD-BLOODED ANIMALS, like reptiles, have body temperatures that change when the weather gets warmer or colder. In contrast, birds and mammals (including people) are warm-blooded, so their temperature always stays about the same (you might feel cold in winter, but your body temperature will stay about 98.6 degrees). For many years, scientists assumed that dinosaurs were cold-blooded—after all, dinosaurs were reptiles.

New evidence and new ideas, however, suggest that dinosaurs may have been warm-blooded, too. One piece of evidence came in 2000, when a group of researchers pointed out that a fossilized heart of *Thescelosaurus*, a dinosaur that looked a bit like *Iguanodon*, had a structure very similar to the structure of a heart from a present-day mammal or bird. Not all scientists agreed, and the debate still goes on to this day.

# Land of Dragons

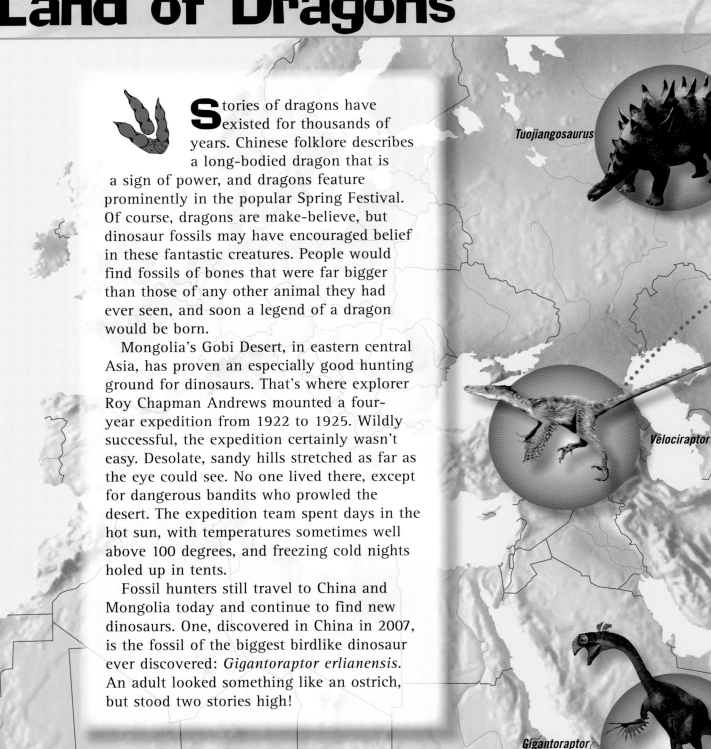

**S**tories of dragons have existed for thousands of years. Chinese folklore describes a long-bodied dragon that is a sign of power, and dragons feature prominently in the popular Spring Festival. Of course, dragons are make-believe, but dinosaur fossils may have encouraged belief in these fantastic creatures. People would find fossils of bones that were far bigger than those of any other animal they had ever seen, and soon a legend of a dragon would be born.

Mongolia's Gobi Desert, in eastern central Asia, has proven an especially good hunting ground for dinosaurs. That's where explorer Roy Chapman Andrews mounted a four-year expedition from 1922 to 1925. Wildly successful, the expedition certainly wasn't easy. Desolate, sandy hills stretched as far as the eye could see. No one lived there, except for dangerous bandits who prowled the desert. The expedition team spent days in the hot sun, with temperatures sometimes well above 100 degrees, and freezing cold nights holed up in tents.

Fossil hunters still travel to China and Mongolia today and continue to find new dinosaurs. One, discovered in China in 2007, is the fossil of the biggest birdlike dinosaur ever discovered: *Gigantoraptor erlianensis*. An adult looked something like an ostrich, but stood two stories high!

*Tuojiangosaurus*

*Velociraptor*

*Gigantoraptor erlianensis*

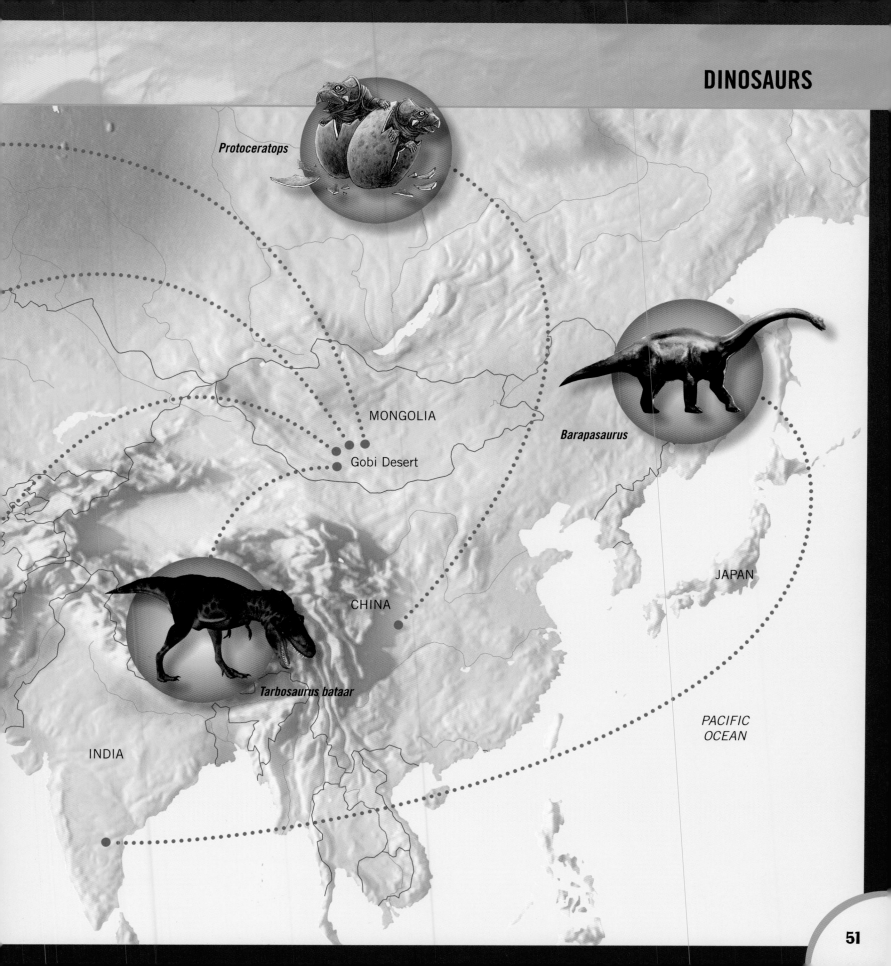

*Protoceratops*

*Barapasaurus*

MONGOLIA

Gobi Desert

JAPAN

CHINA

*Tarbosaurus bataar*

INDIA

PACIFIC
OCEAN

# First Feathers

In 1994, a Chinese farmer split open a rock in Liaoling Province and found a complete fossil of a small dinosaur. Paleontologists studied the amazingly detailed fossil and saw that the dinosaur, named *Sinosauropteryx*, was covered with small feathers. Even though they knew that this 3- to 4-foot-long dinosaur couldn't fly, they were thrilled because it was the very first dinosaur fossil ever discovered with impressions of feathers.

## WHAT'S THE USE?

IF SOME DINOSAURS indeed had feathers, as most paleontologists believe, what did they use them for? Birds use feathers for flight, but dinosaurs couldn't fly. Before you read any further, can you think of a good reason for dinosaurs to have feathers if they didn't fly?

**A male peacock showing off his feathers**

One possibility is that they used them for display, just as many birds do today. Male peacocks, for example, show off to females by fanning out their tails. Another possibility is that dinosaur feathers helped keep the animals warm. When the weather is cold, birds today use their feathers for the same thing. Think about a tiny penguin chick that steps into the frigid temperatures of Antarctica. Without the warmth of its feathers, it would quickly freeze to death.

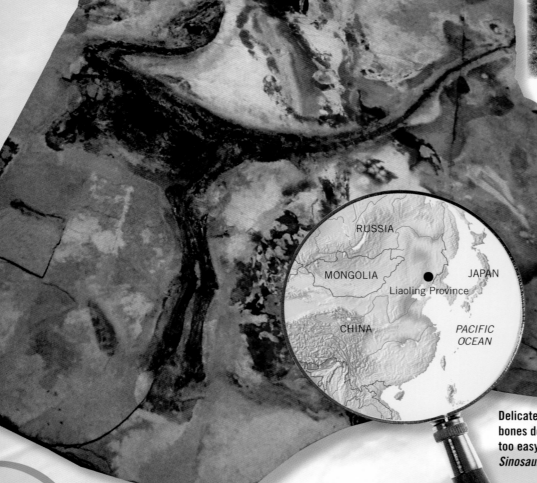

RUSSIA

MONGOLIA

JAPAN

Liaoling Province

CHINA

PACIFIC OCEAN

Delicate structures like feathers and tiny bones don't fossilize well because they're too easy to destroy. That's why fossils like *Sinosauropteryx* are so important.

## From Dinos to Birds

With this discovery, *Sinosauropteryx* became the most primitive dinosaur known to have feathers. Many scientists think it was related to *Compsognathus*, which may have given rise to *Archaeopteryx*, the most primitive known bird. They insist that the little feathers on *Sinosauropteryx* prove once and for all that birds evolved from dinosaurs.

## Feathers or Frill?

A small group of paleontologists, however, disagree. They think that the fibers were actually pieces of a frill, not feathers. So which argument is correct? Scientists probably won't know for certain until they learn more about how feathers fossilize.

*Sinosauropteryx* skeleton

## DINO DATA

### SINOSAUROPTERYX

**SCIENTIFIC NAME:** *Sinosauropteryx*

**MEANING OF NAME:** *Sinosauropteryx* means "Chinese lizard wing" or "Chinese lizard feather," referring to the small feathers on its body.

**SIZE:** 3–4 feet long

**WEIGHT:** 5–7 pounds

**WHEN IT LIVED:** About 130–125 million years ago (Cretaceous)

**DESCRIPTION:** Carnivorous. A small dinosaur with a tail that was longer than the rest of its body. It walked on its two long legs and held its shorter, front arms off the ground. It was the first dinosaur fossil discovered with feathers.

**FIERCE FACTS:** This small theropod was an expert hunter. Scientists learned this when they discovered mammal skull fossils in the belly of one specimen. The skulls belonged to an animal that had a venomous spur on each foot, which means that *Sinosauropteryx* fed on mammals that were very capable of fighting back!

# The Tale of the Egg Thief

**F**or more than seven decades, *Oviraptor* had a most vile reputation: this two-legged, 6-foot-long dinosaur was a baby killer. Scientists believed that it brazenly raided the nests of other dinosaurs, gulping down the defenseless eggs and leaving behind only broken shells. Although it was a colorful story, it couldn't have been further from the truth.

*Oviraptor*

RUSSIA

MONGOLIA

Gobi Desert

CHINA

## Murder at the Nest

Back in the 1920s, famous paleontologist Roy Chapman Andrews and his team went to Mongolia's Gobi Desert. There, they found dozens of fossils from a new, *Triceratops*-like dinosaur that they named *Protoceratops andrewsi*. Much smaller than *Triceratops*, these new dinosaurs seemed to be guarding a nest of eggs—the very first known fossilized dinosaur eggs.

Andrews also discovered a lone fossil of a meat-eating theropod at the nest. Its skull was crushed, and Andrews assumed the theropod was feasting on the *Protoceratops* eggs when it died. The scientists named the theropod *Oviraptor philoceratops*, which means "egg thief with a love for ceratops eggs."

## DINOS BY THE DOZEN

USUALLY PALEONTOLOGISTS have to make educated guesses about what dinosaurs looked like because they have only a few fossil fragments to guide them. Once in a while, however, they find a great variety of fossils from a particular dinosaur. The plant-eating *Psittacosaurus* is one of them. In fact, paleontologists have found so many fossils that they have already identified at least ten different species of *Psittacosaurus* dinosaurs from various parts of Asia. Each was about the size of a deer but usually walked on two legs and had a strong beak. Some species also displayed a large plume on the top of their tails. **This species of *Psittacosaurus* has a frill on its tail. Scientists aren't sure how it used its frill.**

## A Case of Mistaken Identity

It wasn't until 1995 when a group of paleontologists, led by Mark Norell, learned the truth. Norell's research team collected hundreds of additional 8-inch-long eggs in Mongolia, exactly like the eggs Andrews had collected, and found one that proved *Oviraptor*'s innocence. That particular egg contained a fossil of a baby *Oviraptor* dinosaur inside. Andrews had found an *Oviraptor* nest, not a *Protoceratops* nest! After more than seventy years, *Oviraptor*'s reputation was cleared. It wasn't a nasty nest raider after all.

A reconstruction—with an incorrect skull—of *Oviraptor* tending its nest. The skull is actually based on *Citipati,* a related dinosaur often found at nest sites.

## EGG MYSTERIES

SOME DINOSAUR EGGS are round, some are oblong, some are small, some are big (up to 18 inches long!), but all dinosaur eggs are now rocks. So how do scientists see the unborn dinosaurs inside?

One way is to use a tiny chisel to chip away at the egg. Another way is to soak the egg in an acid bath that dissolves the outer layers of the rock (what used to be the egg's shell) and exposes the embryo inside. Scientists can also use computerized axial tomography, or a CAT scan, to see what's inside the egg. Even if they can look inside, though, paleontologists still can't always identify the egg's species.

## Nest Discoveries

Paleontologists have found nests and eggs from various dinosaur species at about 200 different sites around the world. Some of these dinosaurs and the places their eggs were discovered include:

1. **Sauropods** in the Patagonian badlands of Chile and Argentina
2. A **hadrosaur**, a **segnosaur**, and possibly *Saurolophus* and *Therizinosaurus* in the Henan Province of China
3. *Hypacrosaurus* in Alberta, Canada
4. *Orodromeus* in western Montana
5. **Sauropods** in India
6. **Theropods** in Portugal

A model of an opened dinosaur egg

# Asian Terror

**A**sia had its own version of *Tyrannosaurus rex*, a *T. rex* cousin called *Tarbosaurus bataar*. The 40-foot-long *Tarbosaurus* was a bit smaller than *T. rex*, but it was still one of the biggest meat-eating dinosaurs Earth has ever seen. Like *T. rex*, *Tarbosaurus* walked on two massive and very powerful hind legs. It had especially puny arms, each of which ended with two small fingers. Its head, however, was anything but puny. It reached a full 4 feet in length, which is about as long as the average seven-year-old human is tall. Its huge jaws were loaded with about five dozen teeth, some of them almost as long as pencils.

## DINO DATA

### TARBOSAURUS BATAAR

**SCIENTIFIC NAME:** *Tarbosaurus bataar*

**MEANING OF NAME:** *Tarbosaurus* means "terrifying lizard" or "alarming lizard," and *bataar* means "hero."

**SIZE:** 35–40 feet long

**WEIGHT:** About 5 tons

**WHEN IT LIVED:** 70–65 million years ago (Cretaceous)

**DESCRIPTION:** Carnivorous. Walked on two legs with its body bent forward and its two tiny arms held up off the ground. It held its large head 15 to 17 feet above the ground.

**FIERCE FACTS:** *Tarbosaurus* probably lacked *T. rex*'s sharp, 3-D–vision. How did it find its prey? Some scientists think that *Tarbosaurus* had a good sense of smell and hearing, so it could sniff out and listen for prey from a distance.

Above: *Tarbosaurus bataar*

Below: Named for their bright colors in the sunlight, the Flaming Cliffs of the Gobi Desert have yielded many of Mongolia's most amazing fossils.

RUSSIA

MONGOLIA

Gobi Desert

Turpan Basin

CHINA

One of the things that set *Tarbosaurus* apart from *T. rex* was its very rigid jaw. Some paleontologists believe that *Tarbosaurus* may have used this stiff jaw to help it attack and kill some of the biggest animals ever to live on the planet: the enormous, plant-eating titanosaurs, some of which were as long or longer than *Tarbosaurus*. Imagine how the earth itself must have shaken as a desperate titanosaur swung its long tail and neck, trying to flee from the colossal snapping jaws of *Tarbosaurus*!

The skulls of *Tyrannosaurus* (above) and *Tarbosaurus* (below) are very similar. Some paleontologists believe both were actually members of the same genus (*Tyrannosaurus*).

## BUNNYSAURUS?

NOT ALL RELATIVES of *Tyrannosaurus* were big or even meat eaters. In 2002, scientists described a new, 3-foot-long, two-legged dinosaur from Asia. Instead of jaws filled with sharp teeth, this tiny *T. rex* cousin had two big, flat, rabbitlike buck teeth at the front of its mouth. These front teeth, called incisors, gave the dinosaur its name: *Incisivosaurus*. Because its teeth were worn down in the same way that the teeth of today's plant-eating animals are worn, paleontologists think *Incisivosaurus* was probably a plant eater, too.

## Dino Mystery: *Tyrannosaurus* or *Tarbosaurus*?

**CASE OPEN!**

SOME SCIENTISTS question whether *Tarbosaurus bataar* is actually a species of *Tyrannosaurus*. The two looked alike, but they didn't live anywhere near each other. *Tyrannosaurus* was a North American dinosaur and *Tarbosaurus* was an Asian dinosaur. Scientists still aren't certain, so don't be surprised if you see a *Tarbosaurus bataar* on display with the name *Tyrannosaurus bataar*.

# Emerging Africa

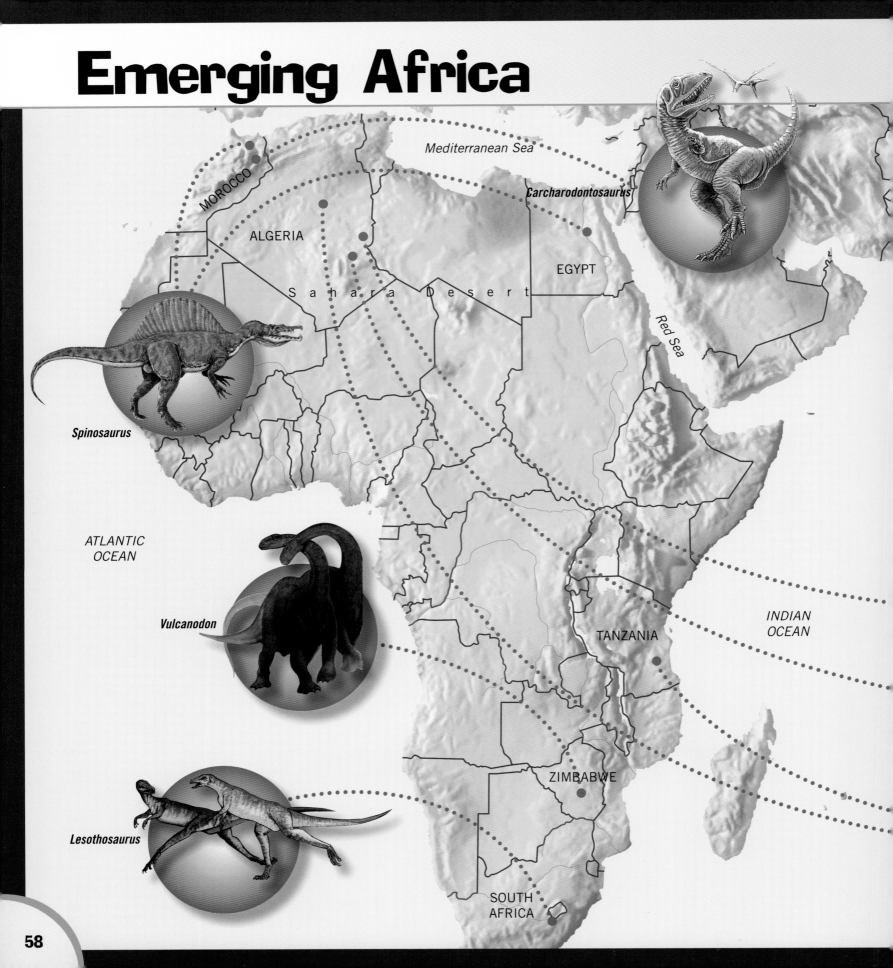

Mediterranean Sea

MOROCCO

ALGERIA

**Carcharodontosaurus**

EGYPT

Red Sea

S a h a r a   D e s e r t

**Spinosaurus**

ATLANTIC
OCEAN

**Vulcanodon**

TANZANIA

INDIAN
OCEAN

**Lesothosaurus**

ZIMBABWE

SOUTH
AFRICA

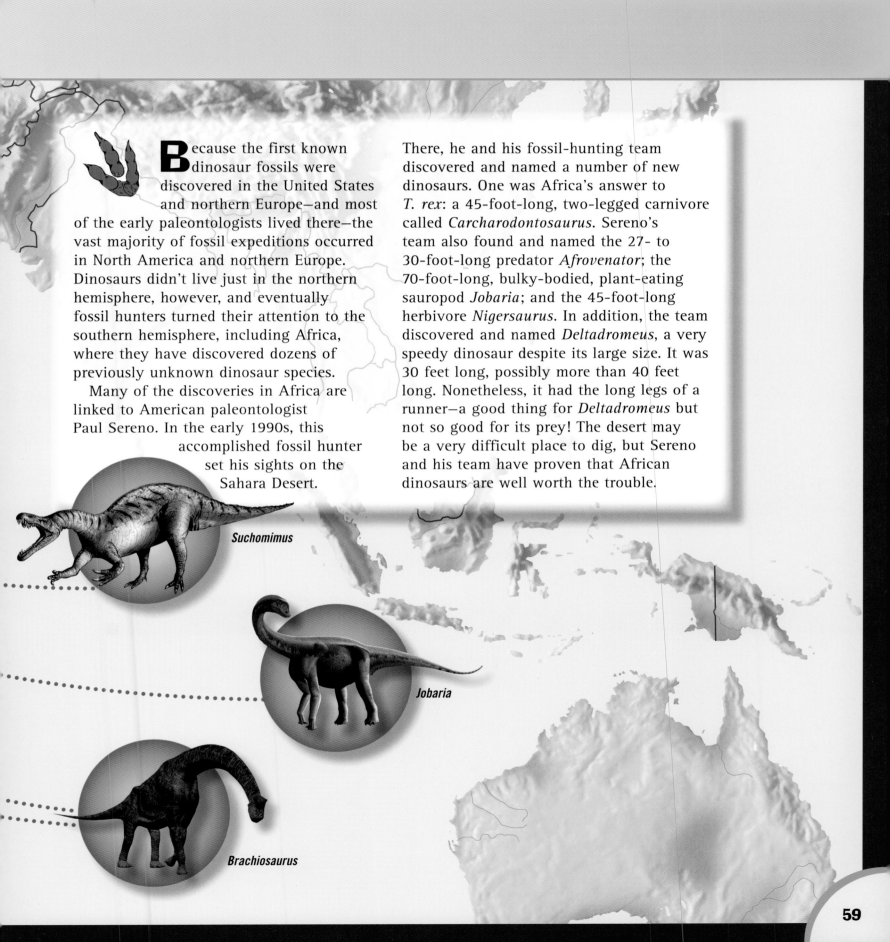

Because the first known dinosaur fossils were discovered in the United States and northern Europe—and most of the early paleontologists lived there—the vast majority of fossil expeditions occurred in North America and northern Europe. Dinosaurs didn't live just in the northern hemisphere, however, and eventually fossil hunters turned their attention to the southern hemisphere, including Africa, where they have discovered dozens of previously unknown dinosaur species.

Many of the discoveries in Africa are linked to American paleontologist Paul Sereno. In the early 1990s, this accomplished fossil hunter set his sights on the Sahara Desert.

There, he and his fossil-hunting team discovered and named a number of new dinosaurs. One was Africa's answer to *T. rex*: a 45-foot-long, two-legged carnivore called *Carcharodontosaurus*. Sereno's team also found and named the 27- to 30-foot-long predator *Afrovenator*; the 70-foot-long, bulky-bodied, plant-eating sauropod *Jobaria*; and the 45-foot-long herbivore *Nigersaurus*. In addition, the team discovered and named *Deltadromeus*, a very speedy dinosaur despite its large size. It was 30 feet long, possibly more than 40 feet long. Nonetheless, it had the long legs of a runner—a good thing for *Deltadromeus* but not so good for its prey! The desert may be a very difficult place to dig, but Sereno and his team have proven that African dinosaurs are well worth the trouble.

*Suchomimus*

*Jobaria*

*Brachiosaurus*

# What Teeth Can Tell

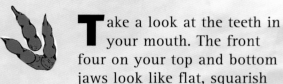

Take a look at the mouth of this *Heterodontosaurus*. The tusk can clearly be seen between the beak and the grinding teeth. *Heterodontosaurus* mostly ate plants, but its odd teeth suggest that its diet may have been a little unusual, too.

Take a look at the teeth in your mouth. The front four on your top and bottom jaws look like flat, squarish blades. These are the incisors. Behind the incisors are pointed teeth, called the canines, and behind the canines are grinding teeth called premolars and molars. Many other mammals have a similar set of varied teeth.

Dinosaurs and most other reptiles, however, usually had only one kind of tooth. The typical meat-eating dinosaur had a mouth full of long, sharp, caninelike teeth, while the typical herbivore had lots of stubbier teeth for eating plants.

*Heterodontosaurus* rears up to reach some cliffside vegetation.

## Different-Toothed Lizard

An exception to the rule came in 1962, when scientists announced that they had found an unusual fossilized skull in South Africa. This small dinosaur had a beak in front that was bordered on each side by two small teeth that resembled pegs. Behind these teeth were large caninelike tusks, and finally a row of cheek teeth that looked something like molars. Scientists named the dinosaur *Heterodontosaurus*, which means "different-toothed lizard."

### DID YOU KNOW?

Some scientists believe that *Heterodontosaurus* may have shared a feature with chipmunks: cheek pouches to store its food!

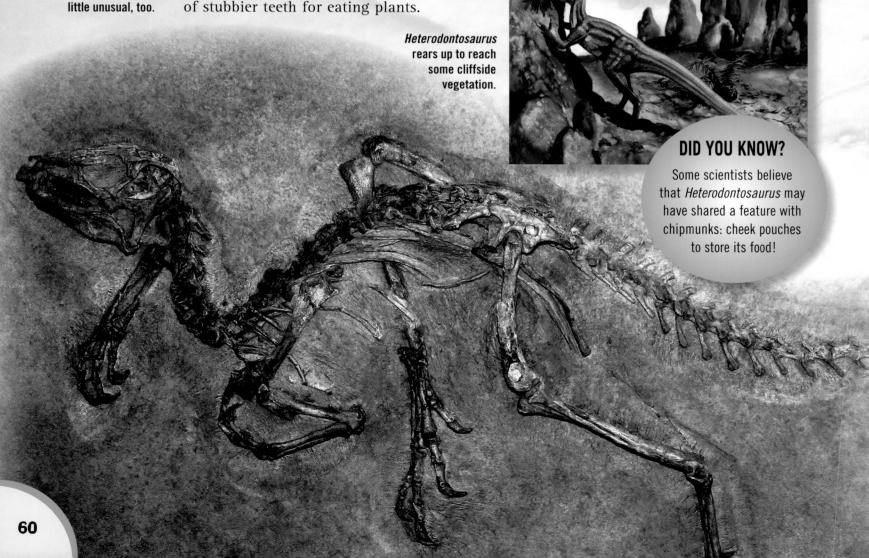

## Dino Mystery: Why Tusks?

CASE OPEN!

THE STRANGE ASSORTMENT of teeth in *Heterodontosaurus* has left scientists scratching their heads. They agree that the dinosaur probably used its beak and front teeth to nip at shrubs or low-growing plants, and its cheek teeth to grind up its food, but why would it need tusks? Paleontologists have suggested several different reasons:

1. When a boar feels threatened, it will defend itself by charging at and slashing its attacker with its tusks. *Heterodontosaurus* may have done the same thing.

2. Maybe only the males had tusks. They may have used them to attract members of the opposite sex.

3. *Heterodontosaurus* dinosaurs may have occasionally added meat to their diet of plants and used the tusks to help them rip into the flesh of small animals. Animals that eat both plants and meat are called omnivores.

A warthog uses its tusk to defend itself from predators, to fight with other warthogs, and to dig for food. *Heterodontosaurus* may have exhibited similar behavior.

DEM. REP. OF THE CONGO
TANZANIA
ANGOLA
ZAMBIA
ZIMBABWE
NAMIBIA
BOTSWANA
MOZAMBIQUE
MADAGASCAR
INDIAN OCEAN
SOUTH AFRICA
Upper Elliot Formation

## HE'S ALL THUMBS

THE STRANGE TEETH of the 3- to 4-foot-long *Heterodontosaurus* weren't this dinosaur's only surprise. It also had five fingers on each hand and two of these—one long, one short—were opposable. Opposable fingers point in the opposite direction from the other fingers. Other dinosaurs didn't have opposable fingers, but humans do: they're called thumbs. If you're not sure how helpful an opposable finger is, spend a few minutes doing things—like flipping through the pages of this book—without using your thumbs!

# Stretching High

In 1900, American paleontologist Elmer Riggs discovered a sauropod skeleton in western Colorado. One pair of its upper leg bones was much longer than the other pair.

Riggs wasn't surprised, because many other sauropods had longer hind legs than front legs. Riggs assumed that this was also true of the new dinosaur. He was wrong. This dinosaur had longer front legs than back legs. That might seem strange, but we have animals with the same setup on Earth today. They are giraffes!

Of course, *Brachiosaurus* would never be confused with a giraffe. For one thing, it grew up to 82 feet long, and its neck alone was longer than a giraffe is tall.

## DID YOU KNOW?

Although *Brachiosaurus* was discovered first in the United States, most *Brachiosaurus* fossils come from Africa. One African *Brachiosaurus*, on display in Berlin, Germany, is the largest mounted skeleton in the world.

This incorrect image shows *Brachiosaurus* underwater. Paleontologists now know it was a land-dwelling dinosaur.

## Dino Mystery: Water Dinosaur?

HOW DID *Brachiosaurus* live? For many years, museums described *Brachiosaurus* as a water animal. Standing on a lake's bottom, *Brachiosaurus* could stretch its long neck up to the surface, pokinge its nostrils out of the water to breathe. Scientists now know that image wasn't the case: this dinosaur lived its life on land. In fact, although a few dinosaurs may have ventured into a lake or a stream once in a while, none of them lived in the water.

**CASE CLOSED!**

## Treetop Browser?

With its long neck stretched upward, *Brachiosaurus* could have reached leaves that were as high as 45 feet above the ground. In other words, if a brachiosaur were to walk into your neighborhood today, it could easily look over the roofs of the houses, including the two-story homes! To hold its head so high, *Brachiosaurus* would have needed an extremely strong heart to pump its blood all the way up its 30-foot-long neck. Without it, the dinosaur would have fainted. Some scientists, however, think that *Brachiosaurus* didn't faint or have a super-powerful heart. Instead, they think that *Brachiosaurus* almost never raised its head above shoulder level and skipped the treetops altogether.

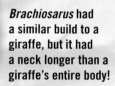

*Brachiosarus* had a similar build to a giraffe, but it had a neck longer than a giraffe's entire body!

## DINO DATA

### BRACHIOSAURUS

**SCIENTIFIC NAME:** *Brachiosaurus*

**MEANING OF NAME:** *Brachiosaurus* means "arm lizard," referring to its front legs, which were longer than its rear legs.

**SIZE:** Up to 82 feet long

**WEIGHT:** 40–60 tons

**WHEN IT LIVED:** 150–145 million years ago (Jurassic)

**DESCRIPTION:** Herbivorous. It walked on four legs. Its uneven legs meant its back was sloped. Compared to the rest of its body, its head was quite small.

**FIERCE FACTS:** Since it was so large, *Brachiosaurus* had to eat a lot. Scientists estimate that it needed more than 400 pounds of leaves and other plant materials every single day. That means *Brachiosaurus* likely spent most of its waking hours doing little but eating.

# Spine-Tingling Dinos

In India, a 21-foot cousin of the crocodile prowls the water. Known as a gharial (or gavial), it emerges from the murky depths, quickly opens its extremely long and narrow jaws, and uses its needlelike teeth to pierce its prey. If that sounds a bit frightening, consider that scientists announced in 2006 that they had found something similar in the dinosaur world: a dinosaur with wicked-looking, spike-toothed jaws. This dinosaur was called *Spinosaurus*, and, unlike a gharial, it walked on two legs and measured 56 feet long. It may have been the largest meat-eating dinosaur ever to live on planet Earth, reaching a full 16 feet longer than even the mighty *T. rex.*

*Spinosaurus*

**Modern gharials have unique, long jaws, the better to catch their unfortunate prey.**

## NEW SPINOSAURS

*BARYONYX* WAS A MEMBER of the spinosaur family. Although *Baryonyx* had the characteristic narrow jaw, it didn't have the family's telltale sail. A fossil hunter discovered the dinosaur in 1983, when he spotted a foot-long, sickle-shaped claw jutting out of the ground in southern England. Paleontologists arrived to uncover the rest of the fossilized bones buried there. To their delight, they found a nearly complete 28-foot-long skeleton. Some scientists now think that this dinosaur may have been a youngster and that the adults may have been even bigger.

In 1996 and 1997, paleontologists announced two new spinosaurs, *Angaturama* and *Irritator*, both of which were discovered in Brazil. Some scientists think that they may actually be the same species, but they don't know for sure because they have only found a single skull from *Irritator* and just part of a skull of *Angaturama*.

## Fish-Eating Menace

Besides its gharial-like jaws, *Spinosaurus* had another feature that made it a particularly dangerous predator. Its arms were much longer and beefier than *T. rex*'s puny pair—the better to reach out and grab its victims. Some scientists think that it ate mainly fish, just as the gharial does, but others think it hunted land animals, too. Either way, the combination of jaws, claws, and big arms made *Spinosaurus* a terrifying killing machine.

*Spinosaurus* tooth

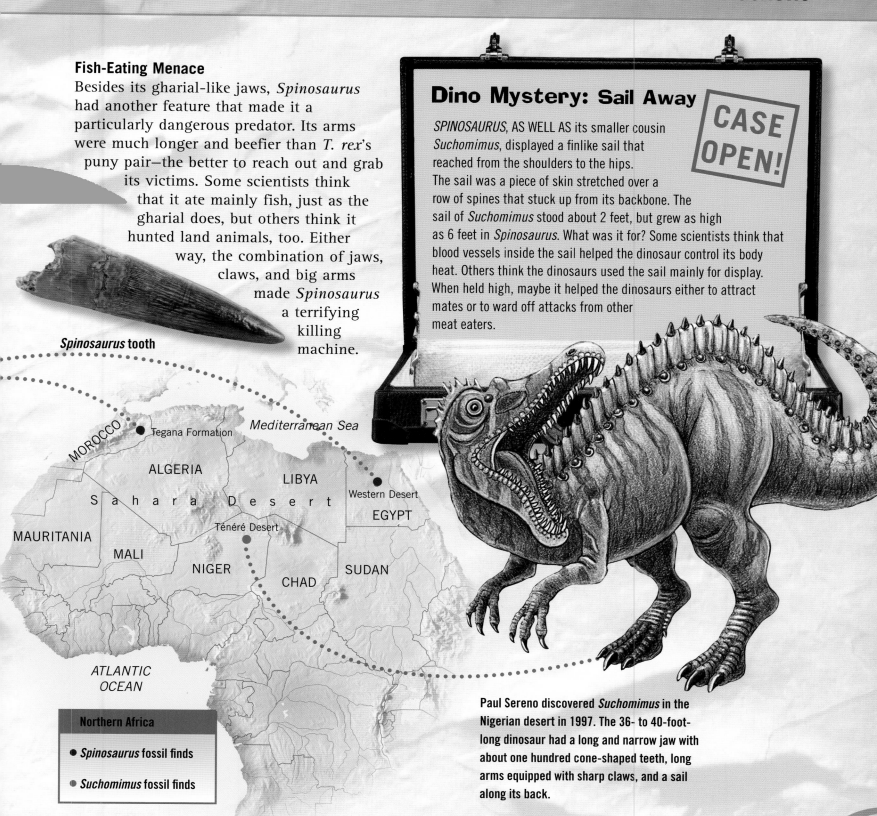

## Dino Mystery: Sail Away

**CASE OPEN!**

*SPINOSAURUS,* AS WELL AS its smaller cousin *Suchomimus,* displayed a finlike sail that reached from the shoulders to the hips. The sail was a piece of skin stretched over a row of spines that stuck up from its backbone. The sail of *Suchomimus* stood about 2 feet, but grew as high as 6 feet in *Spinosaurus.* What was it for? Some scientists think that blood vessels inside the sail helped the dinosaur control its body heat. Others think the dinosaurs used the sail mainly for display. When held high, maybe it helped the dinosaurs either to attract mates or to ward off attacks from other meat eaters.

Mediterranean Sea

MOROCCO • Tegana Formation

ALGERIA

LIBYA

S a h a r a   D e s e r t

Western Desert

EGYPT

MAURITANIA

MALI

Ténéré Desert

NIGER

CHAD

SUDAN

ATLANTIC OCEAN

**Northern Africa**

● *Spinosaurus* fossil finds

● *Suchomimus* fossil finds

Paul Sereno discovered *Suchomimus* in the Nigerian desert in 1997. The 36- to 40-foot-long dinosaur had a long and narrow jaw with about one hundred cone-shaped teeth, long arms equipped with sharp claws, and a sail along its back.

# Way Down Under

For nearly 150 million years, dinosaurs roamed Earth. That's a lot of time to wander— and wander they did, over much of the planet. While that is impressive, humans have inhabited every continent the dinosaurs did in far less time . . . with one major exception. Although a few scientists camp out on Antarctica while working on various research projects, nobody has ever truly colonized this continent, the Earth's largest. But the dinosaurs did. In recent years, scientists have found many dinosaur fossils in Antarctica.

The reason humans have avoided Antarctica is that it is just too cold for people to live there in large numbers. In the Age of Dinosaurs, however, the climate was nothing like it is today. That's because it was farther north, and was actually attached to Australia, India, South America, and Africa for much of its history during the dinosaurs' era. It was also warmer and verdant (meaning it had plenty of trees and plants), making it a good place for dinosaurs millions of years ago, even if it is an uninviting place for humans today.

## Hunter of the South

One of Antarctica's most exciting finds came in 1991, when paleontologists pulled the fossil of a 22-foot-long *Cryolophosaurus* from its icy tomb. This meat-eating theropod stalked its prey some 190 million years ago, in the early Jurassic period. Unusually, *Cryolophosaurus* has a bony crest on its forehead, a little bit like a rooster—if that rooster stood 10 feet high and ate meat for dinner!

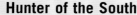

### DID YOU KNOW?

*Cryolophosaurus*'s crest reminded some people so much of 1950s rock star Elvis Presley's distinctive hairstyle that the dinosaur is sometimes jokingly called "Elvisaurus."

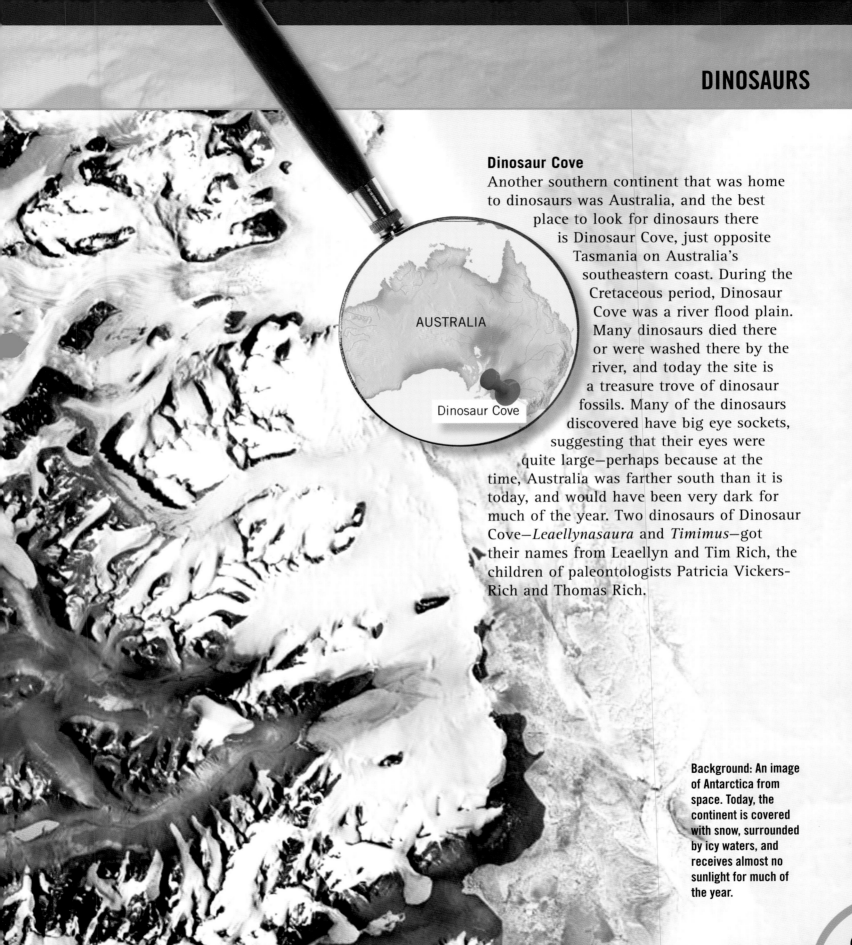

### Dinosaur Cove

Another southern continent that was home to dinosaurs was Australia, and the best place to look for dinosaurs there is Dinosaur Cove, just opposite Tasmania on Australia's southeastern coast. During the Cretaceous period, Dinosaur Cove was a river flood plain. Many dinosaurs died there or were washed there by the river, and today the site is a treasure trove of dinosaur fossils. Many of the dinosaurs discovered have big eye sockets, suggesting that their eyes were quite large—perhaps because at the time, Australia was farther south than it is today, and would have been very dark for much of the year. Two dinosaurs of Dinosaur Cove—*Leaellynasaura* and *Timimus*—got their names from Leaellyn and Tim Rich, the children of paleontologists Patricia Vickers-Rich and Thomas Rich.

AUSTRALIA

Dinosaur Cove

Background: An image of Antarctica from space. Today, the continent is covered with snow, surrounded by icy waters, and receives almost no sunlight for much of the year.

# Find Out More

## WORDS TO KNOW

**ambush.** A hunting technique in which a predator lies hidden in wait for a prey animal to come by, and then surprise attacks.

**ankylosaur.** A type of dinosaur, many of which had armor-covered bodies.

**carnivore.** An organism that eats meat.

**ceratopsian.** A type of dinosaur, many of which had beaked mouths, horns, and frills.

**cold-blooded.** The natural condition of reptiles, fish, and some other animals, in which body temperature changes based on the surrounding temperature.

**decibel**. A measure of how loud a noise is.

**dig**. A fossil-finding activity, in which paleontologists carefully uncover fossils buried in the ground.

**evolution.** Change in a species. Evolution occurs by degrees and over many years.

**extinct.** No longer existing on Earth.

**fossil.** The bones, teeth, or other remains of a plant or an animal that have hardened into rock, or impressions of living matter left in rock.

**geologist.** A scientist who studies rocks and their history.

**Gondwana.** An ancient, massive continent that broke up during the dinosaurs' time and became the modern continents of South America, Africa, Antarctica, and Australia.

**hadrosaur.** A type of duck-billed dinosaur.

**herbivore.** An organism that eats plants.

**Laurasia.** An ancient, massive continent that broke up during the dinosaurs' time and became the modern continents of North America, Europe, and Asia.

**mutation.** A natural but random change that occurs in an individual organism.

**omnivore.** An organism that eats both plants and meat.

**ornithischian.** A dinosaur with so-called "bird hips." All dinosaurs are either ornithischians or saurischians.

**paleontologist.** A fossil expert.

**periods.** Spans of time in Earth history. Dinosaurs lived during the periods called the Triassic (250 to 203 million years ago), Jurassic (203 to 144 million years ago), and Cretaceous (144 to 65 million years ago).

**predator.** An animal that eats other animals.

**prey.** An animal that is eaten by other animals.

**quarry.** A place where people dig for stone. Dinosaur bones are often discovered in quarries as people dig into the rock.

**radioactivity.** A naturally occurring quality of some chemicals, which can help scientists determine the age of fossils.

**reptile.** A cold-blooded animal with a backbone, scaly skin, and lungs for breathing. Reptiles include snakes, lizards, turtles, crocodiles, and dinosaurs, among others.

**saurischian.** A dinosaur with so-called "lizard hips." All dinosaurs are either saurischians or ornithischians.

**sauropod.** A plant-eating saurischian. Most were large, long-necked dinosaurs that walked on four legs and had long tails.

**scavenger.** An animal that eats other animals who have died already from old age, disease, predation, or any other cause. Vultures are well-known scavengers today.

**scientific name.** A two-word name scientists give to organisms. The first word is called the genus name and the second is called the species name. The name is typically based on the Greek or Latin language, and is used by scientists worldwide.

**spinosaur.** A type of theropod dinosaur characterized by a sail or similar structure along the spine and a crocodilelike snout.

**Tethys Sea.** An ocean that existed on prehistoric Earth.

**theropod.** A meat-eating, saurischian dinosaur.

**titanosaur.** A group of sauropods that includes some of the biggest dinosaurs ever known.

**tyrannosaur.** A theropod family whose members walked on two legs and typically had tiny arms.

**warm-blooded.** The natural condition of birds and mammals, in which the animal's body temperature stays the same even when the surrounding temperature changes.

## WEB SITES TO VISIT

### The Scholastic Dinosaur

http://teacher.scholastic.com/ activities/dinosaurs/

Filled with kids' games and quizzes related to dinosaurs.

### How Stuff Works

http://animals.howstuffworks.com/ dinosaurs

Provides descriptions of many dinosaurs and investigates how scientists learn about these ancient animals.

### The American Museum of Natural History

http://www.amnh.org/exhibitions/ dinosaurs/

Explains how scientists piece together clues to learn about dinosaurs. It also includes information about a wide range of different dinosaur species.

### The University of California Museum of Paleontology

http://www.ucmp.berkeley.edu/ diapsids/dinosaur.html

Separates dinosaur fact from dinosaur fiction and answers some commonly asked questions.

### "Zoom Dinosaurs"

http://www.enchantedlearning. com/subjects/dinosaurs/

Covers many dinosaur species, along with articles on how dinosaurs lived. Dinosaur evolution, extinction, and fossil discoveries are also covered.

## BOOKS TO READ

Barrett, Paul. *National Geographic Dinosaurs*, National Geographic Children's Books, 2001.

Bingham, Caroline. *First Dinosaur Encyclopedia*, DK Publishing, 2007.

Halls, Kelly Milner. *Dinosaur Mummies: Beyond Bare-Bone Fossils*, Darby Creek Publishing, 2003.

Holtz, Thomas. *Dinosaurs: The Most Complete, Up-to-Date Encyclopedia for Dinosaur Lovers of All Ages*, Random House Books for Young Readers, 2007.

Lessem, Don. *Scholastic Dinosaur A to Z*, Scholastic Reference, 2003.

Malam, John. *Dinosaur Atlas: An Amazing Journey Through a Lost World*, DK Children, 2006.

Paul, Gregory. *The Scientific American Book of Dinosaurs*, St. Martin's Griffin, 2003.

Sloan, Christopher. *Feathered Dinosaurs*, National Geographic Children's Books, 2000.

Sloan, Christopher. *Bizarre Dinosaurs: Some Very Strange Creatures and Why We Think They Got That Way*, National Geographic Children's Books, 2008.

# Index

## A

Africa, 12, 29, 59, 62
  Sahara Desert, 59
*Afrovenator*, 59
Age of Dinosaurs, 10, 13, 66
*Allosaurus*, 28, 29, 30, 31
American Museum of Natural
    History, 24
Andrews, Roy Chapman, 50, 54
*Angaturama*, 64
ankylosaur, 34, 35
*Ankylosaurus*, 35
Antarctica, 6, 66
*Apatosaurus*, 9, 26, 27, 30
*Archaeopteryx*, 43, 46, 47, 53
Argentina, 18, 20, 21, 55
    Valley of the Moon, 14, 16, 17
*Argentinosaurus*, 18, 19, 20
Asia, 40, 50, 54, 57
*Astrodon*, 6
Australia
    Dinosaur Cove, 67

## B

*Barapasaurus*, 51
*Baryonyx*, 64
Belgium, 43
Berlin, Germany, 62
birds, relationship to dinosaurs,
    8, 32, 37, 46, 47, 49, 53
Bonaparte, José F., 18
brachiosaur, 63
*Brachiosaurus*, 19, 59, 62, 63
Brazil, 64
Brown, Barnum, 40
Buckland, William, 44

## C

*Camarasaurus*, 26, 27
*Camptosaurus*, 42

Canada, 12
  Alberta, 55
  Edmonton, 8, 36
*Carcharodontosaurus*, 58, 59
*Carnotaurus*, 21
Carolini, Ruben, 20
*Centrosaurus*, 39
ceratopsian, 39
*Ceratosaurus*, 28
Chicago Field Museum of Natural
    History, 41
Chile, 55
China, 12, 29, 50
    Henan Province, 55
    Liaoling Province, 52
*Citipati*, 55
*Coelophysis*, 24, 25
*Compsognathus*, 47, 53
Cope, Edward Drinker, 27
Coria, Rodolfo, 18
Cretaceous period, 10, 11, 13, 67
*Cryolophosaurus*, 66
Crystal Palace, 45
Cuvier, Georges, 44

## D

*Deinonychus*, 32, 33, 48
*Deltadromeus*, 59
*Diplodocus*, 26
dromaeosaur, 32, 33
duck-billed dinosaur (*see also*
    hadrosaur), 6, 22, 36

## E

*Edmontonia*, 35
*Edmontosaurus*, 8, 36
England, 43, 44, 48, 64
*Eoraptor*, 16, 17
*Euoplocephalus*, 34
Europe, 43, 49, 59

## F

Fernbank Museum of Natural
    History, 18
fossilization, 12

## G

Germany, 46
*Giganotosaurus*, 20, 21
*Gigantoraptor*, 50
Gondwana, 11, 46

## H

hadrosaur (*see also* duck-billed
    dinosaur), 36, 37, 55
*Hadrosaurus*, 6, 22
Hawkins, Benjamin
    Waterhouse, 45
Herrera, Victorino, 17
*Herrerasaurus*, 10, 16, 17
*Heterodontosaurus*, 60, 61
*Huayangosaurus*, 29
Huincul, Argentina, 18
*Hylaeosaurus*, 43
*Hypacrosaurus*, 55
*Hypsilophodon*, 42

## I

*Iguanodon*, 42, 43, 48, 49
*Incisivosaurus*, 57
India, 55
*Irritator*, 64
Ischigualasto (*see* Argentina,
    Valley of the Moon)

## J

*Jobaria*, 59
Jurassic period, 10, 11, 26, 28,
    30, 66